Duino Elegies

Duineser Elegien

Aus dem Besitz der Fürstin
Marie von Thurn und Taxis-Hohenlohe

RILKE

Duino Elegies

translated by Stephen Cohn

illustrations by Elisabeth Frink
preface by Peter Porter

CARCANET

First published in 1989 by
Carcanet Press Limited
Alliance House
Cross Street
Manchester M2 7AQ

The German text of *Duineser Elegien* is published
by Insel Verlag, Frankfurt am Main (first published 1923).

British Library Cataloguing in Publication Data

Rilke, Rainer Maria, *1875-1926*
  Duino elegies.
  I. Title   II. Duineser Elegien, *English*
  831'.8

  ISBN 0-85635-836-2 hardback
  ISBN 0-85635-837-1 paperback

The Publisher acknowledges financial assistance from
the Arts Council of Great Britain

Typeset in 10pt Palatino by Bryan Williamson, Manchester
Printed in England by SRP Ltd., Exeter

Contents

I have been given very generous help in my work on the *Elegies*:
by Ray Ockenden of Wadham College, Oxford; by Peter Porter;
and by Corbet Stewart of Queen Mary College, London. I also
wish to thank Parimal, from whose suggestion this whole project
grew.

I dedicate this translation to my wife Laura, and to these friends
and helpers.

S.C.

Preface

THE *Duino Elegies*, and indeed Rilke himself, are the victims of their own enormous success. Perhaps no poems in another European language have made so dramatic and sustained an impact on English-speaking readers in this century. But just writing that last sentence comes up with the rub: these *echt-Deutsch* poems, embodying perhaps the most remarkable leap of the German imagination since the heyday of Romanticism, are known to generations of their admirers in English translations of varying degrees of loyalty to the original. One must be fair about this – some poetry, even the most idiosyncratic, still lives in what you might call the sinopia of its ideas. The *Duino Elegies* and the poems of Cavafy are prominent examples of such a special shelf-life. The second point to stress is that the *Elegies* first gained currency in a version of quite special authority – that by Stephen Spender and J.B. Leishman – which has gone on being a steady seller since the Hogarth Press first issued it in the 1930s. Dozens of rival translations have appeared on the scene since this one, but none has replaced it in public esteem. Leishman had been translating Rilke throughout the 1930s and his and Spender's success owes something to the timing of their publication: the Anglo-Saxon psyche was passing through one of its conversions – away from positivism and towards mysticism, you might say. True, Modernism had been imposed on the British and American consciousness by Eliot and Pound, but that movement was essentially French. Not everyone in these islands or in the States took kindly to such Frenchness, especially when it was filtered through scraps of Provençal and made Dante pre-eminent over Shakespeare, and it became decidedly quirky when the *Cantos* appeared on the scene. Rilke, dead prematurely in 1926, appeared in his newly-run-up English dress as a Messiah. Here was something different from the 'aesthetic' tones of Pound and Eliot: it was almost case-history poetry, it seemed to speak with the accents of Freud (an Austrian voice like the hardly-known Kafka's or Musil's). At the same time it was unswervably serious. Perhaps Rilke's most noticeable stylistic tic to his English-speaking readers was his use of personification. This was not in itself new to English poetry – Shakespeare teems with it – but it amounted in Rilke's verse, particularly in the *Duino Elegies*, to a new way of writing. As in dreams, things lost their hard edges, categories leaked into each other – landscape became anthropomorphic.

9

Matched to Rilke's Tarnhelm-like fluidity was a syntax at once magisterial and serpentine: the German genius for forming and reforming words like carriages coupled to an ever-changing train was turned from a dangerous bore to a newfangled attraction. Perhaps not since Milton or the Arnold of 'The Scholar Gypsy' had English readers encountered such a dragon's-tail to a poem as the one which winds down at the end of the Fifth Elegy. Suddenly, German became the rage.

In Britain the 1930s was the age of Auden as well as the age of Rilke. The influence of Rilke on Auden is a complex subject. Concepts like 'To settle in the village of the heart, / My darling, can you bear it?' seem Rilke-like, and there is Auden's tribute among the knowing couplets of 'New Year Letter'.

And RILKE, whom *die Dinge* bless,
The Santa Claus of loneliness.

. . .

Then, as I start protesting, with
The air of one who understands,
He puts a RILKE in my hands.
'You know the *Elegies*, I'm sure –
O Seligkeit der Kreatur
Die immer bleibt im Schoosse – womb
In English is a rhyme to tomb.'

Yet I suspect that the vogue for all things German, Berlin, boys, Brecht, Communism, the mesmerising progress of Fascism, the cult of sun and undress – which Auden and Isherwood substituted for an obligatory admiration for that French culture which had previously been the intellectual mode among English writers – had more to do with Rilke's popularity than any practical influence his poetry exerted on English poets. The irony of this popularity would not have been lost on Rilke had he lived to see it. He was, after all, a paid-up Anglophobe; he had lived in Paris and he admired French art. But once Rilke had conquered the Anglo-Saxon imagination his triumph never faltered, and has not done so to this day.

It is not my intention to write an essay on Rilke as a poet but rather to introduce Stephen Cohn's remarkable English versions of the *Duino Elegies*. And yet, more must still be said about Rilke's appeal to readers of English. Why have so many translators addressed themselves to the task of rendering him into English? A sort of new Rilke is reborn in English dress, one not always recognised by German-speakers. I have often mentioned my enthusiasm for Rilke's poetry to Germans and Austrians only to receive in return their severe reservations about his stature and performance. Had I read Stefan George, Dehmel, Trakl, Morgenstern, Celan, Ingeborg Bachmann, Bobrowski, etc.? Rilke's German is too difficult for us possessors of opera-German to be able to do more than read him haltingly in the original. But he is not the sort of poet you can consult like a table of logarithms – you must read him headlong, as his syntax and imagination demand that you do. So, willy nilly, you must read him in English. Here an important codicil to the great poetic will should be entered: if poetry is that which gets lost in translation, nevertheless poetic shapes are independent of the quiddities of language. The way Rilke dramatises the *Gestalt*, though new in English, is just as exciting in our tongue as it is in the German. Freud can do the same. Thus the job of the translator of Rilke is to seek the underlying structure of Rilke's thought-and-feeling, and only then to cope with its clothing in words. Of course, this secondary task is baffling enough, since Rilke's German is as rich and involved as a tropical jungle. Rilke's case is, in this respect, different from Freud's, of whom it has been said that he writes the most lucid German since Luther. Rilke's language serves poetic insight and is not ideas-carrying prose. (Much German prose could be described as ideas-concealing.) It is that Rilke's mind has got into our minds, and thence into our sensibility and language. Hundreds of poets who know little Rilke know 'Archaic Torso of Apollo' with its injunction, 'You must change your life', 'The Panther', 'Orpheus. Eurydice. Hermes', and the famous opening of the First Elegy. 'Orpheus. Eurydice. Hermes' must have been translated as often as Valéry's 'Le Cimetière Marin' and frequently just as unsatisfactorily. Thus, when we tackle the *Duino Elegies* we are coming to terms with a set of chimerical shadows, the bits of Rilke which have got into our blood and worked in it like Auden's 'filter-passing predators', as well as attempting a formidable technical task with language.

It has taken Stephen Cohn more than three years of hard work and constant revision to complete his translation. During this period I have had many sessions with him, going over certain passages again and again seeking eloquent English for Rilke's elusive poetic vision. The real Rilke poem seems to hover before you like Plato's already-existing ideal form. Conjuring it down on the page becomes the job of a shaman. One thing you cannot do – and some of Rilke's translators have done it – is to find a loosely colloquial Procrustean form – say, unrhymed three-line stanzas – and pour all the protean poetry of the *Elegies* into these containers like a confectioner making sweets. Your translation must have grandeur, essential size in its component parts, and speed to catch the marvellous twists of Rilke's imagination. Seeking an English form for each Elegy which reproduces the technical devices of the German will not work. On the other hand, the English should match the German at least in outline, and should not diminish or over-elaborate. Cohn has met all these requirements, in my view, and has added a natural eloquence of his own which makes his versions of the *Elegies* the most flowing and organic of those I have read. The rhythms are difficult: how to match Rilke's 'onwardness' in a language which does not dovetail together as happily as German does. Grinding dissonances and rhythmical thumps are strong drawbacks in the Spender/Leishman translations. And he has made sense of those weird German yokings which if translated literally sound like Bedlam-in-the-computer in English. He has the first and most valuable of qualifications as a translator: he fell in love with the poems and wanted to remake them in his own diurnal language. German was his first tongue, and it is to that loved but rejecting culture he has returned on a pilgrimage in these translations.

There are notes on the translations provided at the back of this book, and I shall confine myself to making only a few points here. In the First Elegy, the translator's solution to the conflict of possibilities when rendering the famous opening provides a key to his method throughout the poems. At no time is Rilke's meaning betrayed, yet this meaning comes to us in a nimbus of light. Rilke is curiously argumentative for a poet, and Cohn gives him to us in his full combativeness, but never at the expense of that eloquence which is argument's other. And there is no fudging of Rilke's Angels: they are present in full Pentecostal dress. Nor are Rilke's romantic exhortations denied their oracular bossiness. Strangeness is made natural but not neutered – you will find 'the young man, the one sired by a neck on a nun' in his proper place in the Fifth Elegy, and you will wonder at the beautifully gentle winding down at the end of this incomparable poem:

> And suppose they found it;
> suppose they found it with an audience around them
> of the un-numberable and silent dead:
> would not those dead then scatter
> their last, their carefully-hoarded ever-kept-secret
> coins of happiness – eternal legal tender –
> upon that couple who at last
> are truthfully smiling, upon that ineffable carpet
> ... finally stilled?

For the numinous Eighth Elegy – Rilke's summoning of 'the sadness of the creatures' and of their beauty also – Cohn employs iambic pentameter, the most natural of English metres, since Rilke uses it too. English iambics sound different from German, but his matching is both felicitous and precise. The Tenth Elegy, the bitterest, finds him ready to catch Rilke's humour, as in the 'Sex Life of Money' section. The apotheosis of this extraordinary poem is splendidly rendered.

No matter how many versions of the *Duino Elegies* you have you will need Cohn's. I cannot quite parody Goethe and state that here the untranslatable is at last translated, but it is almost the case. These are fine poems in English, and they are Rilkean poems too. The *Elegies* belonged from the start to the German-speaking world and were not just the property of the Princess of Thurn and Taxis. We English-speakers have claimed them as a bequest to us as well.

Peter Porter

Introduction

ON A day in January 1912, preoccupied and pacing the bastions of Castle Duino, the wind howling and the Adriatic raging beneath him, Rilke seemed to hear a voice which called to him from the storm:

> *Wer, wenn ich schriee, hörte mich denn aus der Engel Ordnungen?*
> Who, if I cried out, would hear me – among the Angel
>   hierarchies?

He copied these words into his notebook and from this dramatic moment his life's mission, as he saw it, truly began. The First and Second Elegies followed immediately, but the Elegy cycle was not to be completed until 1922. Rilke believed that the *Elegies* were his *Auftrag*: the work he had been given to perform in life. For ten bitter years it must have seemed that he might never complete them.

In the February of 1922, at the little Château de Muzot, in the Valais, during an amazing three weeks Rilke experienced a frenzy of achievement: he 'completed' the *Elegies* and then wrote the Elegie des Saltimbanques to replace the original Fifth Elegy. But in addition he began and completed the two sequences of the *Sonnets to Orpheus*; a total of 55 sonnets (as they now stand) which bear close relation to the *Elegies*. Rilke felt himself rewarded and achieved. He died soon after, on 29 December 1926.

Rilke's language and imagery and the Rilkean legend have passed into the English literary inheritance. Auden, Rilke's most influential English disciple, frequently paid homage to him, as in these lines which tell of the *Elegies* and of their difficult and chancy genesis:

> When all our apparatus of report
> Confirms the triumph of our enemies,
> Our frontier crossed, our forces in retreat,
> Violence pandemic like a new disease,
>
> And Wrong a charmer everywhere invited,
> When Generosity gets nothing done,
> Let us remember those who looked deserted:

Tonight in China let me think of one

Who for ten years of drought and silence waited
Until in Muzot all his powers spoke
And everything was given once for all.

Awed, grateful, tired, content to die, completed,
He went out in the winter night to stroke
That tower as one pets an animal.
                    (W.H. Auden, 'Sonnets from China', XIX, 1936)

The *Elegies* raise a number of questions. What is their subject?
Is it primarily the creative act – the life, death, being, transforma-
tions of art, of poetry itself? Does Rilke take Life for his subject?
Or is it primarily the Life of Art? I believe that the *Elegies* must
be seen as a poem about the experience of being human, which
includes the experience of art. To an artist as deeply engaged as
Rilke the distinctions fade and Life and Art dissolve in one
another. Every salmon is generically a fish: every fish, then, *some-
thing* of a salmon.

How reliable are the *Elegies* – not as poetry but as a system of
belief? Perhaps to question them in this way is to misunderstand
their purpose. Certainly, the *Elegies* preach; but is this their prime
intention? The mythic and heroic figures of the *Elegies* which live
in the landscape Rilke provides are no more important than are
the birds, bats, chariots, trees, gentians, gnats and violins. They
are described as sharing World with Rilke himself and with our-
selves – and with Gods and Angels and lovers, as well as with
various forms of Terror. 'We are the bees of the invisible,' Rilke
wrote in the famous letter to Hulewicz, his Polish translator,
'frantically we gather in the honey of the visible – to store it in
the great golden hive of the invisible.' (*Briefe aus Muzot*, 1921-1926)
It is from a life experience turned inward that Rilke fashions
images which are sometimes terrifying; images which themselves
become various kinds of truth. The poem shows much; explains
little; legislates unreliably if at all.

For the shape of the *Elegies* is above all dialectical: no sooner
does affirmation seem to triumph over despair than the balance
is reversed. Life and death. Stasis and transformation. Loss and
gain. All things are shown in terms of one another. The tentative
synthesis offered at the close of the Tenth Elegy, as if spoken
by a kind and visionary child, says some of it. But the greater
synthesis is stated by the entire poem, the poem as a whole;
implicit in its flux and contradictions; reconciliations.

16

Rilke has a habit of referring us, not backwards to what has already been explained, but forward towards image and exposition still to come – so that it seems inevitable that there has been so much argument over 'interpretation'. Again and again he chooses words and patterns of syntax which break the stream of his content into tributaries and sometimes reverse their flow. This is because he belongs to the genus of muse-poets Graves describes in *The White Goddess*. Rilke distrusts, as every muse-poet, every anti-Apollonian, must, the cerebral, the self-aware, the 'designed' or 'invented'. He elevates the child above the adult, praises the animal at the expense of the human, and apostasises from Christian faith and institutions. His Muse is not the Goddess but the Angel, yet Rilke is without doubt an inheritor of the tradition of invocation, secrecy and magic that Graves describes.

Translators of poetry tend either towards the depressive or the manic. On the one hand lies the anxious, the scrupulous, above all the *literal* dot-for-dot translation of words from their original language. One at a time. Or, on the other hand, a more relaxed, more 'creative' attack leads to something that is not quite an original poem, but not quite a translation either.

In this version (it is at the same time 'version', 'translation', 'imitation': it has to be) I have above all attempted to make poetry in English from the German text; to make something that possessed its own integrity and life; something faithful but not something tame. Where I have felt that English asked for an image different from the German, I have first hesitated and then made changes.

The accompanying German text largely follows that of the *Sämtliche Werke* (Insel Verlag, Frankfurt am Main, 1955-1966). Rilke's own intentions in regard to layout and punctuation were not always clear. There are small but important variations between one published edition and another, and I have in seven cases returned to the format of earlier editions.

Line references, in the notes on the translation, are to the German text only. Explanation and discussion of the *Elegies* themselves has been kept relatively sparse: some degree of difficulty and ambiguity of interpretation in the original is certainly present because that is what Rilke intended. But his *Elegies* become steadily richer and more meaningful when one returns to them again and again, and at each reading there is less that seems difficult.

Stephen Cohn

Die erste Elegie

WER, wenn ich schriee, hörte mich denn aus der Engel
Ordnungen? und gesetzt selbst, es nähme
einer mich plötzlich ans Herz: ich verginge von seinem
stärkeren Dasein. Denn das Schöne ist nichts
als des Schrecklichen Anfang, den wir noch grade ertragen,
und wir bewundern es so, weil es gelassen verschmäht,
uns zu zerstören. Ein jeder Engel ist schrecklich.
Und so verhalt ich mich denn und verschlucke den Lockruf
dunkelen Schluchzens. Ach, wen vermögen
wir denn zu brauchen? Engel nicht, Menschen nicht,   10
und die findigen Tiere merken es schon,
daß wir nicht sehr verläßlich zu Haus sind
in der gedeuteten Welt. Es bleibt uns vielleicht
irgendein Baum an dem Abhang, daß wir ihn täglich
wiedersähen; es bleibt uns die Straße von gestern
und das verzogene Treusein einer Gewohnheit,
der es bei uns gefiel, und so blieb sie und ging nicht.
    O und die Nacht, die Nacht, wenn der Wind voller Weltraum
uns am Angesicht zehrt –, wem bliebe sie nicht, die ersehnte,
sanft enttäuschende, welche dem einzelnen Herzen   20
mühsam bevorsteht. Ist sie den Liebenden leichter?
Ach, sie verdecken sich nur miteinander ihr Los.
    Weißt du's *noch* nicht? Wirf aus den Armen die Leere
zu den Räumen hinzu, die wir atmen; vielleicht daß die Vögel
die erweiterte Luft fühlen mit innigerm Flug.

The First Elegy

WHO, if I cried out, might hear me – among the ranked Angels?
Even if One suddenly clasped me to his heart
I would die of the force of his being. For Beauty is only
the infant of scarcely endurable Terror, and we
are amazed when it casually spares us.
   Every Angel is terrible.
And so I check myself, choke back my summoning
black cry. Who'll help us then? Not Angels,
not Mankind; and the nosing beasts soon scent
how insecurely we're housed in this signposted World.
And yet a tree might grow for us upon some hill
for us to see and see again each day. Perhaps
we have yesterday's streets. Perhaps we keep
the pampered loyalty of some old habit
which loved its life with us – and stayed, never left us.
   But, oh, the nights – those nights when the infinite wind
eats at our faces! Who is immune to the night, to Night,
ever-subtle, deceiving? Hardest of all to the lonely,
Night, is she gentler to lovers? Oh, but they only
use one another as cover, to hide what awaits them.
   Do you *still* not know it? Throw that emptiness
out of your arms and into the air that we breathe:
does it widen the sky for the birds – add zest to their flight?

Ja, die Frühlinge brauchten dich wohl. Es muteten manche
Sterne dir zu, daß du sie spürtest. Es hob
sich eine Woge heran im Vergangenen, oder
da du vorüberkamst am geöffneten Fenster,
gab eine Geige sich hin. Das alles war Auftrag.   30
Aber bewältigtest du's? Warst du nicht immer
noch von Erwartung zerstreut, als kündigte alles
eine Geliebte dir an? (Wo willst du sie bergen,
da doch die großen fremden Gedanken bei dir
aus und ein gehn und öfters bleiben bei Nacht.)
Sehnt es dich aber, so singe die Liebenden; lange
noch nicht unsterblich genug ist ihr berühmtes Gefühl.
Jene, du neidest sie fast, Verlassenen, die du
so viel liebender fandst als die Gestillten. Beginn
immer von neuem die nie zu erreichende Preisung;   40
denk: es erhält sich der Held, selbst der Untergang war ihm
nur ein Vorwand, zu sein: seine letzte Geburt.
Aber die Liebenden nimmt die erschöpfte Natur
in sich zurück, als wären nicht zweimal die Kräfte,
dieses zu leisten. Hast du der Gaspara Stampa
denn genügend gedacht, daß irgendein Mädchen,
dem der Geliebte entging, am gesteigerten Beispiel
dieser Liebenden fühlt: daß ich würde wie sie?
Sollen nicht endlich uns diese ältesten Schmerzen
fruchtbarer werden? Ist es nicht Zeit, daß wir liebend   50
uns vom Geliebten befrein und es bebend bestehn:
wie der Pfeil die Sehne besteht, um gesammelt im Absprung
mehr zu sein als er selbst. Denn Bleiben ist nirgends.

Stimmen, Stimmen. Höre, mein Herz, wie sonst nur
Heilige hörten: daß sie der riesige Ruf
aufhob vom Boden; sie aber knieten,
Unmögliche, weiter und achtetens nicht:
so waren sie hörend. Nicht daß du *Gottes* ertrügest
die Stimme, bei weitem. Aber das Wehende höre,
die ununterbrochene Nachricht, die aus Stille sich bildet.   60
Es rauscht jetzt von jenen jungen Toten zu dir.
Wo immer du eintratst, redete nicht in Kirchen
zu Rom und Neapel ruhig ihr Schicksal dich an?

Yes, *you* were needed. Every springtime needed you.
Even stars relied on your witnessing presence
when a gathering wave surged from the past – or when
some violin utterly offered itself
as you passed by a half-opened window. All this was your mission.
Did you discharge it? Were you not ever distracted
by anticipation? As if all Creation existed
only to signal a mistress? (Where would you keep her?
With those great foreign Conjectures coming and going
by night as by day?)
                                    Yet, if you must, sing of lovers –
those famous passions, still not immortal enough:
those whom you almost envied – those who were cheated,
abandoned. You thought them more ardent than those
who are quenched and requited. Ever again recommence
your unachievable task: you must praise!
For the Hero, remember, lives on. To the Hero
death is no more than his recentest birth; his reason for being.
And Nature herself, exhausted, takes lovers back
into herself – as if there were strength to achieve them,
but only one time... And you...?
Have you sufficiently thought about Gaspara Stampa;
remembered that somewhere a woman whose lover had left her
might, reaching beyond herself, pray: Let me be as she was...?
Is it not time for these oldest of heartaches, now
at last, to bear fruit for us? Is it time that, still loving, we learned
how to leave our beloved and, trembling, endure it?
As an arrow endures the bowstring and focused on flight
becomes... more than itself. Nothing stays still.

Voices. The voices. Oh, my heart, hear,
as once only The Holy could hear, the huge cry
which raised them up from the depths. Who could believe
that, unheeding, they never once rose from their knees?
Not by far could you bear to hear God's voice. Yet, listen:
borne on the wind, in voices made of the silence,
those who died young endlessly whisper a message.
Wherever you go, in churches of Rome or of Naples,
does not their destiny softly address you?

Oder es trug eine Inschrift sich erhaben dir auf,
wie neulich die Tafel in Santa Maria Formosa.
Was sie mir wollen? Leise soll ich des Unrechts
Anschein abtun, der ihrer Geister
reine Bewegung manchmal ein wenig behindert.

Freilich ist es seltsam, die Erde nicht mehr zu bewohnen,
kaum erlernte Gebräuche nicht mehr zu üben,   70
Rosen, und andern eigens versprechenden Dingen
nicht die Bedeutung menschlicher Zukunft zu geben;
das, was man war in unendlich ängstlichen Händen,
nicht mehr zu sein, und selbst den eigenen Namen
wegzulassen wie ein zerbrochenes Spielzeug.
Seltsam, die Wünsche nicht weiterzuwünschen. Seltsam,
alles, was sich bezog, so lose im Raume
flattern zu sehen. Und das Totsein ist mühsam
und voller Nachholn, daß man allmählich ein wenig
Ewigkeit spürt. – Aber Lebendige machen   80
alle den Fehler, daß sie zu stark unterscheiden.
Engel (sagt man) wüßten oft nicht, ob sie unter
Lebenden gehn oder Toten. Die ewige Strömung
reißt durch beide Bereiche alle Alter
immer mit sich und übertönt sie in beiden.

Schließlich brauchen sie uns nicht mehr, die Früheentrückten,
man entwöhnt sich des Irdischen sanft, wie man den Brüsten
milde der Mutter entwächst. Aber wir, die so große
Geheimnisse brauchen, denen aus Trauer so oft
seliger Fortschritt entspringt – : *könnten* wir sein ohne sie?   90
Ist die Sage umsonst, daß einst in der Klage um Linos
wagende erste Musik dürre Erstarrung durchdrang,
daß erst im erschrockenen Raum, dem ein beinah göttlicher
                    Jüngling
plötzlich für immer enttrat, das Leere in jene
Schwingung geriet, die uns jetzt hinreißt und tröstet und hilft.

Or, as that day in Santa Maria Formosa,
a tablet compels your heightened attention.
What do they ask me to do? To wipe out those feelings
of outrage – which hamper their spirit's free flight.

How strange... no longer to live upon Earth!... Strange
no more to depend upon practices only just learned
nor to expect from roses – nor to expect
from any thing of exceptional wonder – interpretation
of Mankind's future. No longer to live
as we used to, our hands ever frightened. To throw
away the names we were given: toys that have broken.
Strangely – to lose our desire for things we desire.
To see all those things which once stood related
freed of connection – fluttering in space!
And Death is demanding; we have much to atone for
before little by little we begin to taste of eternity.
Yet... the living are wrong when they distinguish so clearly:
Angels, it's said, are often unsure
whether they pass among living or dead.
Ever-racing, the current whirls each generation
through both those kingdoms. In both it outsounds them.

In the end, the early-departed need us no longer,
gradually weaned from things of our World
as the babe grows away from the gentle
breasts of its mother. But we? Who have such deep need
of great mysteries, we who rarely progress without mourning
... can we do without them?
                                        Does it mean nothing, the myth
in which earliest Music in mourning for Linos
dares to invade desolate wilderness? A young man
not far from immortal, suddenly gone! And forever!
And the shocked emptiness for the first time
resounds with what ravishes, comforts and aids us.

Die zweite Elegie

JEDER Engel ist schrecklich. Und dennoch, weh mir,
ansing ich euch, fast tödliche Vögel der Seele,
wissend um euch. Wohin sind die Tage Tobiae,
da der Strahlendsten einer stand an der einfachen Haustür,
zur Reise ein wenig verkleidet und schon nicht mehr furchtbar;
(Jüngling dem Jüngling, wie er neugierig hinaussah).
Träte der Erzengel jetzt, der gefährliche, hinter den Sternen
eines Schrittes nur nieder und herwärts: hochauf-
schlagend erschlüg uns das eigene Herz. Wer seid ihr?

Frühe Geglückte, ihr Verwöhnten der Schöpfung,   10
Höhenzüge, morgenrötliche Grate
aller Erschaffung, – Pollen der blühenden Gottheit,
Gelenke des Lichtes, Gänge, Treppen, Throne,
Räume aus Wesen, Schilde aus Wonne, Tumulte
stürmisch entzückten Gefühls und plötzlich, einzeln,
Spiegel, die die entströmte eigene Schönheit
wiederschöpfen zurück in das eigene Antlitz.

Denn wir, wo wir fühlen, verflüchtigen; ach wir
atmen uns aus und dahin; von Holzglut zu Holzglut
geben wir schwächern Geruch. Da sagt uns wohl einer: 20
ja, du gehst mir ins Blut, dieses Zimmer, der Frühling

The Second Elegy

EVERY Angel is terror. I know it, yet still, alas!
I must sing you – you, great near-deadly birds
of the soul! Where have they gone, the days of Tobias
when one of those brilliant ones stood at the door
of the unexceptional house? Dressed for the journey
he was not at all terrible, a youth to the youth
who eagerly spied him. But should the Archangel –
dangerous, masked by the stars – should *he* tread
but a step lower and closer we should be struck down
by our hammering hearts. What *are* you?

Fortune's favourites, early-successful,
destiny-pampered; you stand as our very peaks
and our summit, seem crested and touched
by the rose of Creation; pollen of Godhead's own flowering;
limbs of the light; paths, stairways, thrones,
realms of pure being; emblazoned delight;
riots of sense's enchantments: and, of a sudden, alone –
you are mirrors: you pour out your beauty
but your faces gather it back to yourselves.

For whenever we feel – we evaporate;
we breathe ourselves, breathless, away; from ember to ember
burn with less fragrance. And when someone tells us:
Yes, my heart beats for you only; this room

füllt sich mit dir... Was hilfts, er kann uns nicht halten,
wir schwinden in ihm und um ihn. Und jene, die schön sind,
o wer hält sie zurück? Unaufhörlich steht Anschein
auf in ihrem Gesicht und geht fort. Wie Tau von dem Frühgras
hebt sich das Unsre von uns, wie die Hitze von einem
heißen Gericht. O Lächeln, wohin? O Aufschaun:
neue, warme, entgehende Welle des Herzens – ;
weh mir: wir *sinds* doch. Schmeckt denn der Weltraum,
in den wir uns lösen, nach uns? Fangen die Engel   30
wirklich nur Ihriges auf, ihnen Entströmtes,
oder ist manchmal, wie aus Versehen, ein wenig
unseres Wesens dabei? Sind wir in ihre
Züge soviel nur gemischt wie das Vage in die Gesichter
schwangerer Frauen? Sie merken es nicht in dem Wirbel
ihrer Rückkehr zu sich. (Wie sollten sie's merken.)

Liebende könnten, verstünden sie's, in der Nachtluft
wunderlich reden. Denn es scheint, daß uns alles
verheimlicht. Siehe, die Bäume *sind*; die Häuser,
die wir bewohnen, bestehn noch. Wir nur   40
ziehen allem vorbei wie ein luftiger Austausch.
Und alles ist einig, uns zu verschweigen, halb als
Schande vielleicht und halb als unsägliche Hoffnung.

Liebende, euch, ihr ineinander Genügten,
frag ich nach uns. Ihr greift euch. Habt ihr Beweise?
Seht, mir geschiehts, daß meine Hände einander
inne werden oder daß mein gebrauchtes
Gesicht in ihnen sich schont. Das gibt mir ein wenig
Empfindung. Doch wer wagte darum schon zu sein?
Ihr aber, die ihr im Entzücken des andern   50
zunehmt, bis er euch überwältigt
anfleht: nicht *mehr* – ; die ihr unter den Händen
euch reichlicher werdet wie Traubenjahre;
die ihr manchmal vergeht, nur weil der andre
ganz überhandnimmt: euch frag ich nach uns. Ich weiß,

28

and this springtime contain only you – Why, what of it?
He still cannot hold us; we disappear in him, around him.
And those who are beautiful...? Oh, what might restrain them?
Appearance ceaselessly comes and goes in their faces...
As morning dew rises we lose what was ours...
the heat steams from us as from dishes uncovered.
What of our laughter, what of the watchfulness;
of the heart's surges, building, fading...?
...Alas, that *is* us.
Does then the cosmos in which we are gradually melting
not take a touch of our flavour? Not even
a taste of us? And the Angels, do they truly gather up
only their own... what flows out from them?
Isn't some of our essence, sometimes, by chance,
gathered up with it? Haven't we become
part of their nature? Just as women in pregnancy
share the same look, unknown to themselves,
                 a look of abstraction...?
(Why should they notice, caught in the whirling return into *self*?)

Lovers, if they knew how, might speak wondrously
under the night's silent air... It is as though
all things concealed us. See, our trees *stand*
and the houses we live in endure. Only we,
we alone drift past all of it – as if air
no more than changed places with air. And all things
conspire to silence us – we who embarrass them
yet remain, perhaps, their unsayable hope.

Lovers: you who suffice for each other might answer
questions about us. You clasp one another:...
                 what's your authority?
Listen: sometimes my lonely hands reach out
to possess one another; sometimes my used-up face
comforts itself in them. These things touch my senses... but who
could find in them franchise for daring to *be*...?
Yet you, who increase each by the other one's rapture
until, overcome, each begs the other: Enough!... You,
in the hands of each other growing to greater abundance
than vines in the greatest of years; you
who may perish, quite overpowered by your lover;
it is you that I ask about us. I know

29

ihr berührt euch so selig, weil die Liebkosung verhält,
weil die Stelle nicht schwindet, die ihr, Zärtliche,
zudeckt; weil ihr darunter das reine
Dauern verspürt. So versprecht ihr euch Ewigkeit fast
von der Umarmung. Und doch, wenn ihr der ersten 60
Blicke Schrecken besteht und die Sehnsucht am Fenster
und den ersten gemeinsamen Gang, *ein* Mal durch den Garten:
Liebende, *seid* ihrs dann noch? Wenn ihr einer dem andern
euch an den Mund hebt und ansetzt – : Getränk an Getränk:
o wie entgeht dann der Trinkende seltsam der Handlung.

Erstaunte euch nicht auf attischen Stelen die Vorsicht
menschlicher Geste? war nicht Liebe und Abschied
so leicht auf die Schultern gelegt, als wär es aus anderm
Stoffe gemacht als bei uns? Gedenkt euch der Hände,
wie sie drucklos beruhen, obwohl in den Torsen die Kraft steht, 70
Diese Beherrschten wußten damit: so weit sind wirs,
dieses ist unser, uns *so* zu berühren; stärker
stemmen die Götter uns an. Doch dies ist Sache der Götter.

Fänden auch wir ein reines, verhaltenes, schmales
Menschliches, einen unseren Streifen Fruchtlands
zwischen Strom und Gestein. Denn das eigene Herz übersteigt uns
noch immer wie jene. Und wir können ihm nicht mehr
nachschaun in Bilder, die es besänftigen, noch in
göttliche Körper, in denen es größer sich mäßigt.

why your touching's so fervent: those caresses preserve!
You safeguard forever the spot which your gentle hands cover
and, beating beneath, you feel the true pulse of permanence...
so that every embrace is almost to promise: Forever!
But yet: after those first frightened glances; when
yearning has stood at the window; and after
that first walk (once through the garden together)...
are you still the same, Lovers? When you raise
lips to the lips of the other, drinking each other
...strange, how those drinkers depart from it all.

Careful in gesture, did not the figures upon
Attic stelae amaze you? Is not Love, is not Parting
laid on the shoulders so lightly as to suggest
they are utterly different from ours? Consider the hands:
they press lightly, for all the strength of the torsos.
Those disciplined people knew this: We reach only so far.
This much is ours: to touch one another like this.
The Gods bear upon us more fiercely – but that is a matter for Gods.

Might not we find somewhere secret – simple and decent
and human? Some strip of our own fertile ground
to lie between river and rock? For, as theirs did,
our own heart exceeds us: we cannot trace it in pictures
               (which tame it);
nor in godlike sculptures which yet more control it.

Die dritte Elegie

EINES ist, die Geliebte zu singen. Ein anderes, wehe,
jenen verborgenen schuldigen Fluß-Gott des Bluts.
Den sie von weitem erkennt, ihren Jüngling, was weiß er
selbst von dem Herren der Lust, der aus dem Einsamen oft,
ehe das Mädchen noch linderte, oft auch als wäre sie nicht,
ach, von welchem Unkenntlichen triefend, das Gotthaupt
aufhob, aufrufend die Nacht zu unendlichem Aufruhr.
O des Blutes Neptun, o sein furchtbarer Dreizack.
O der dunkele Wind seiner Brust aus gewundener Muschel.
Horch, wie die Nacht sich muldet und höhlt. Ihr Sterne,   10
stammt nicht von euch des Liebenden Lust zu dem Antlitz
seiner Geliebten? Hat er die innige Einsicht
in ihr reines Gesicht nicht aus dem reinen Gestirn?

Du nicht hast ihm, wehe, nicht seine Mutter
hat ihm die Bogen der Braun so zur Erwartung gespannt.
Nicht an dir, ihn fühlendes Mädchen, an dir nicht
bog seine Lippe sich zum fruchtbarern Ausdruck.
Meinst du wirklich, ihn hätte dein leichter Auftritt
also erschüttert, du, die wandelt wie Frühwind?
Zwar du erschrakst ihm das Herz; doch ältere Schrecken   20
stürzen in ihn bei dem berührenden Anstoß.
Ruf ihn... du rufst ihn nicht ganz aus dunkelem Umgang.

The Third Elegy

ONE thing to sing the beloved: how different, alas! to sing
of that secret and wicked river-god of our blood!
What can that young man, marked from afar by a girl,
know of that Lord of Desire; of that implacable head
bursting again and again – up from the fathomless depths!
Still unconsenting, often... often as if she were *nothing*...
stirring the night awake to unending uproar.
O the god of our blood, his barbed, cruel trident;
O ominous wind from his breast of spiralling seashell!
Listen, the night moulds itself into caverns and tunnels.
O stars, does not a lover's delight in the face of his mistress
come straight from you? Does not his knowledge
        of her shining features
flow to him out of the night's shining stars?

Alas, it was not you, his mother,
who bent the bow of his eyebrows to urgent expectancy.
Nor is it your presence, maiden so moved by him,
curving his lip to such a fervent expression.
You, whose footfall is light as the dawn's...
can you really believe that the sound of your gentle approach
could so discompose him? Yes, you touched fear in his heart,
but terror itself came rushing back too, with that touch.
Call to him: it isn't easy to hold him back
from those bitter engagements; yet that's what he wants

Freilich, er *will*, er entspringt; erleichtert gewöhnt er
sich in dein heimliches Herz und nimmt und beginnt sich.
Aber begann er sich je?
Mutter, *du* machtest ihn klein, du warsts, die ihn anfing;
dir war er neu, du beugtest über die neuen
Augen die freundliche Welt und wehrtest der fremden.
Wo, ach, hin sind die Jahre, da du ihm einfach
mit der schlanken Gestalt wallendes Chaos vertratst? 30
Vieles verbargst du ihm so; das nächtlich verdächtige Zimmer
machtest du harmlos, aus deinem Herzen voll Zuflucht
mischtest du menschlichern Raum seinem Nacht-Raum hinzu.
Nicht in die Finsternis, nein, in dein näheres Dasein
hast du das Nachtlicht gestellt, und es schien wie aus Freundschaft.
Nirgends ein Knistern, das du nicht lächelnd erklärtest,
so als wüßtest du längst, *wann* sich die Diele benimmt...
Und er horchte und linderte sich. So vieles vermochte
zärtlich dein Aufstehn; hinter den Schrank trat
hoch im Mantel sein Schicksal, und in die Falten des Vorhangs 40
paßte, die leicht sich verschob, seine unruhige Zukunft.

Und er selbst, wie er lag, der Erleichterte, unter
schläfernden Lidern deiner leichten Gestaltung
Süße lösend in den gekosteten Vorschlaf – :
schien ein Gehüteter... Aber *innen*: wer wehrte,
hinderte innen in ihm die Fluten der Herkunft?
Ach, da *war* keine Vorsicht im Schlafenden; schlafend,
aber träumend, aber in Fiebern: wie er sich einließ.
Er, der Neue, Scheuende, wie er verstrickt war,
mit des innern Geschehns weiterschlagenden Ranken 50
schon zu Mustern verschlungen, zu würgendem Wachstum,
    zu tierhaft
jagenden Formen. Wie er sich hingab – . Liebte.
Liebte sein Inneres, seines Inneren Wildnis,
diesen Urwald in ihm, auf dessen stummem Gestürztsein
lichtgrün sein Herz stand. Liebte. Verließ es, ging die
eigenen Wurzeln hinaus in gewaltigen Ursprung,
wo seine kleine Geburt schon überlebt war. Liebend
stieg er hinab in das ältere Blut, in die Schluchten,

and so he wins free and escapes them. Unburdened, he learns
to live in his secret retreat, his place in your heart;
there he takes up his self and begins it.

   Did he ever *really* begin it?
Mother: you made his model...it was you who began him;
new, even to you. Bending your body
over the eyes newly-opened, you were a whole world familiar.
Where did they go? the years when your slender figure,
alone, stood in the path of weltering chaos?
You shielded him from so much; made innocent
the bedroom which night had turned sinister; brought from the
              store
of your sheltering heart a human dimension to night-space.
And the candle, you placed it...not out there in the dark,
you brought it close to shine on your nearness, shining in
              friendship.
Each unexplained sound, you would smile and explain it
as if you had known in advance every creak of the boards...
and he heard you; he relaxed, reassured. So many portents
demanded your tender alertness; his cloaked Fate,
tall by the wardrobe – and in folds of the curtains his Future,
fugitive, restless.

And the boy? He feels his heavy eyelids dissolving
in the sweet foretaste of sleep which you conjure. Lies there
unburdened...and seems one protected. Yet
who can ward off, who safeguards his future?
Who stills the whirlpool raging inside him, the tempest of Origin?
Oh, how the child – sleeping; dreaming; feverish –
lets himself get carried completely away!
Such a new creature; so timid; already so deep entangled
in vine and creeper – all the activity writhing inside him
starting to weave itself into pattern; looping and choking;
predatory...animal. Yet how completely he gave himself to it.
Loved. Doted on all that wildness
inside him. Loved and gave himself up to exploring
the primitive beckoning forest within him; and over
its silent decay his shining green heart stood.
Loved. Loved it and left it behind him, outgrowing
his own roots...reaching for urgent *beginning*. Loving,
he finds himself wading in ancestral blood, goes down
into chasms where Terrors lie, sated; gorged

wo das Furchtbare lag, noch satt von den Vätern. Und jedes
Schreckliche kannte ihn, blinzelte, war wie verständigt.　　　　60
Ja, das Entsetzliche lächelte... Selten
hast du so zärtlich gelächelt, Mutter. Wie sollte
er es nicht lieben, da es ihm lächelte. *Vor* dir
hat ers geliebt, denn, da du ihn trugst schon,
war es im Wasser gelöst, das den Keimenden leicht macht.

Siehe, wir lieben nicht, wie die Blumen, aus einem
einzigen Jahr; uns steigt, wo wir lieben,
unvordenklicher Saft in die Arme. O Mädchen,
dies: daß wir liebten *in* uns, nicht Eines, ein Künftiges, sondern
das zahllos Brauende; nicht ein einzelnes Kind,　　　　70
sondern die Väter, die wie Trümmer Gebirgs
uns im Grunde beruhn; sondern das trockene Flußbett
einstiger Mütter – ; sondern die ganze
lautlose Landschaft unter dem wolkigen oder
reinen Verhängnis – : *dies* kam dir, Mädchen, zuvor.

Und du selber, was weißt du – , du locktest
Vorzeit empor in dem Liebenden. Welche Gefühle
wühlten herauf aus entwandelten Wesen. Welche
Frauen haßten dich da. Was für finstere Männer
regtest du auf im Geäder des Jünglings? Tote　　　　80
Kinder wollten zu dir... O leise, leise,
tu ein liebes vor ihm, ein verläßliches Tagwerk, – führ ihn
nah an den Garten heran, gib ihm der Nächte
Übergewicht...
　　　　　　Verhalt ihn...

with the flesh of his fathers. They know him; nodding and winking;
        sharing the secret.
The Unspeakable smiled at him – you, his mother, were
never as tender; how could he not answer with love
the thing that lay smiling...?
Loved it before even you. It was present
from the first day you bore him, dissolved in the waters
        that carried his making.

Understand this: we do not love as flowers love,
all out of one single year. Whenever, wherever we love
the ageless juice rises...fills us, suffuses our limbs.
Dearest: that we might love, hold within us,
not the awaited One, but the Many;
their ferment too great to be numbered. Not one single child
but all fathers; like the ruins of mountains
they lie buried within us. Not one child
but the dry river-bed of long-ago mothers
– and all silent landscapes, whether their skies
show cloudless or stormy. Dearest: all this was before you.

As for yourself? Why then...it was you
who teased out prehistory from deep in your lover:
what emotion, from creatures long-gone, burst up into light!
What of the women who loathed you, and what of the spirits
of darkhearted men you roused in the veins of the young?
Dead children sought you.
But softly, now, softly: it is time
to do him some kindness, time to stand by him;
time to lead him close up to the garden...to help him
outbalance the night...to contain him.

Die vierte Elegie

O BÄUME Lebens, o wann winterlich?
Wir sind nicht einig. Sind nicht wie die Zug-
vögel verständigt. Überholt und spät,
so drängen wir uns plötzlich Winden auf
und fallen ein auf teilnahmslosen Teich.
Blühn und verdorrn ist uns zugleich bewußt.
Und irgendwo gehn Löwen noch und wissen,
solang sie herrlich sind, von keiner Ohnmacht.

Uns aber, wo wir eines meinen ganz,
ist schon des andern Aufwand fühlbar. Feindschaft   10
ist uns das Nächste. Treten Liebende
nicht immerfort an Ränder, eins im andern,
die sich versprachen Weite, Jagd und Heimat.
    Da wird für eines Augenblickes Zeichnung
ein Grund von Gegenteil bereitet, mühsam,
daß wir sie sähen; denn man ist sehr deutlich
mit uns. Wir kennen den Kontur
des Fühlens nicht, nur was ihn formt von außen.
    Wer saß nicht bang vor seines Herzens Vorhang?
Der schlug sich auf: die Szenerie war Abschied.   20
Leicht zu verstehen. Der bekannte Garten,

The Fourth Elegy

O TREES of Life: how shall we know your Winter?
The migrant birds can tell the seasons...we,
kept ignorant and left behind, must force
ourselves belatedly upon a wind
and come down hard on some uncaring pond.
In fullest flower we know our withering:
yet somewhere still the lions walk and in
their proud prime know themselves invincible.

And we, when we are quite resolved upon
one thing, can sense the other...tugging us
away. Conflict is seldom far from us.
Why, even lovers frequently transgress
their boundaries – who never fail to vow
that they'll provide wide prairies – hunting – home.
    And so, for just a lightning sketch, this ground
of contradiction's carefully prepared;
all is deliberately made very clear
for us. Still we mistake our feelings, their
true shape: we see them only from outside.
    Is there a man who never watched in dread
before the lowered curtain of his heart...?
It rises...to reveal a stage all set
for: *Parting*. Not difficult to understand.
And, trembling slightly, that familiar garden.

und schwankte leise: dann erst kam der Tänzer.
Nicht *der*. Genug! Und wenn er auch so leicht tut,
er ist verkleidet, und er wird ein Bürger
und geht durch seine Küche in die Wohnung.
Ich will nicht diese halbgefüllten Masken,
lieber die Puppe. Die ist voll. Ich will
den Balg aushalten und den Draht und ihr
Gesicht aus Aussehn. Hier. Ich bin davor.
Wenn auch die Lampen ausgehn, wenn mir auch   30
gesagt wird: Nichts mehr –, wenn auch von der Bühne
das Leere herkommt mit dem grauen Luftzug,
wenn auch von meinen stillen Vorfahrn keiner
mehr mit mir dasitzt, keine Frau, sogar
der Knabe nicht mehr mit dem braunen Schielaug:
Ich bleibe dennoch. Es gibt immer Zuschaun.

Hab ich nicht recht? Du, der um mich so bitter
das Leben schmeckte, meines kostend, Vater,
den ersten trüben Aufguß meines Müssens,
da ich heranwuchs, immer wieder kostend   40
und, mit dem Nachgeschmack so fremder Zukunft
beschäftigt, prüftest mein beschlagnes Aufschaun, –
der du, mein Vater, seit du tot bist, oft
in meiner Hoffnung innen in mir Angst hast,
und Gleichmut, wie ihn Tote haben, Reiche
von Gleichmut, aufgibst für mein bißchen Schicksal,
hab ich nicht recht? Und ihr, hab ich nicht recht,
die ihr mich liebtet für den kleinen Anfang
Liebe zu euch, von dem ich immer abkam,
weil mir der Raum in eurem Angesicht,   50
da ich ihn liebte, überging in Weltraum,
in dem ihr nicht mehr wart...: wenn mir zumut ist,
zu warten vor der Puppenbühne, nein,
so völlig hinzuschaun, daß, um mein Schauen
am Ende aufzuwiegen, dort als Spieler
ein Engel hinmuß, der die Bälge hochreißt.
Engel und Puppe: dann ist endlich Schauspiel.
Dann kommt zusammen, was wir immerfort

A pause. But then: the Dancer. Not that one.
Enough! However gracefully he moves,
he changes role and costume. Now he is
the Solid Citizen: goes through the kitchen,
walks around his house.
                                   I cannot bear
these masquerading masks, half full
of nothing! Give me a puppet... full at least
of stuff! Better the sewn-up body, wires
and shallow show-face! Ready and waiting. *Now*.
And if the lights go down... and even if
they come and say: That's all. And even if
that empty greyness drifts, comes breathing from
the stage, and not a single one of all
my silent forbears stays with me. No wife.
Not the boy with the squint and his brown eyes.
I shan't leave. I shall stay. I'll stay and watch.

Am I not right? You knew the bitter taste
of life, Father, because you tasted mine
(that muddy ferment of compulsion in me):
as I grew older kept on tasting still,
and, troubled by the after-flavour of
that unknown destiny, you tried to look
into my clouded gaze. My Father, who
are often, since you died, alive in me
and anxious in my hope: your own
serenity – only the Dead possess
a kingdom so serene – you offer up
to ransom my own little piece of Fate.
Am I not right? And all of you, who loved
that tiny germ of love I had for you,
from which I always turned aside again,
because the space I'd loved in all your eyes
dissolved in cosmic Space: and you were gone...
...Am I not right, then, that I feel impelled
to linger by the puppet-stage... but, more:
I stare so hungrily that, in the end,
to satisfy my gaze an Angel's called
and plays his part... wrenches those dolls to life!
Angel and Puppet: now – at last – a *play*!
Now all can fuse together, all that we

41

entzwein, indem wir da sind. Dann entsteht
aus unsern Jahreszeiten erst der Umkreis   60
des ganzen Wandelns. Über uns hinüber
spielt dann der Engel. Sieh, die Sterbenden,
sollten sie nicht vermuten, wie voll Vorwand
das alles ist, was wir hier leisten. Alles
ist nicht es selbst. O Stunden in der Kindheit,
da hinter den Figuren mehr als nur
Vergangnes war und vor uns nicht die Zukunft.
Wir wuchsen freilich, und wir drängten manchmal,
bald groß zu werden, denen halb zulieb,
die andres nicht mehr hatten als das Großsein.   70
Und waren doch in unserem Alleingehn
mit Dauerndem vergnügt und standen da
im Zwischenraume zwischen Welt und Spielzeug,
an einer Stelle, die seit Anbeginn
gegründet war für einen reinen Vorgang.

Wer zeigt ein Kind, so wie es steht? Wer stellt
es ins Gestirn und gibt das Maß des Abstands
ihm in die Hand? Wer macht den Kindertod
aus grauem Brot, das hart wird, – oder läßt
ihn drin im runden Mund so wie den Gröps   80
von einem schönen Apfel?... Mörder sind
leicht einzusehen. Aber dies: den Tod,
den ganzen Tod, noch *vor* dem Leben so
sanft zu enthalten und nicht bös zu sein,
ist unbeschreiblich.

divide by merely being here. And now
our seasons take their place in the great round
of change that changes endlessly: now
can the Angel...above us and beyond us...
play his part!
                Consider the dying: do they
not come at last to guess the hollowness
of everything that we engage in here?
Nothing is what it is! O childhood hours,
whose presences possessed behind them more
than Past...when Future did not lie before us.
We grew and grew, and even sometimes made
haste to be fully-grown; half for the sake
of those grown-ups...who owned so little else.
Left to our own devices we were still
made glad enough by all the things that stayed
eternally the same, so that we lived
within a borderland: between the hard World
and our objects of Delight; inhabited
a place that always, from the very first,
had been reserved for innocent events.

Who will show us what children really are?
Who sets them in the constellations, puts
a yardstick to tell *difference* in their hands?
Who moulds the deaths of children, who makes death
from that grey bread; leaves it to harden...? Or
sucks at it, roundmouthed, the core that's left
of some sweet apple? Easy enough, to see
into the hearts of murderers, but this:
to bear all death, the whole of death; death even
before life; and gently, without rancour
to keep it, contain it,
is terrible beyond all language.

Die fünfte Elegie

Frau Hertha Koenig zugeeignet

WER aber *sind* sie, sag mir, die Fahrenden, diese ein wenig
Flüchtigern noch als wir selbst, die dringend von früh an
wringt ein *wem* – *wem* zuliebe
niemals zufriedener Wille? Sondern er wringt sie,
biegt sie, schlingt sie und schwingt sie,
wirft sie und fängt sie zurück; wie aus geölter,
glatterer Luft kommen sie nieder
auf dem verzehrten, von ihrem ewigen
Aufsprung dünneren Teppich, diesem verlorenen
Teppich im Weltall.   10
Aufgelegt wie ein Pflaster, als hätte der Vorstadt-
Himmel der Erde dort wehegetan.
                              Und kaum dort,
aufrecht, da und gezeigt: des Dastehns
großer Anfangsbuchstab..., schon auch, die stärksten
Männer, rollt sie wieder, zum Scherz, der immer
kommende Griff, wie August der Starke bei Tisch
einen zinnenen Teller.

Ach und um diese
Mitte, die Rose des Zuschauns:
blüht und entblättert. Um diesen   20
Stampfer, den Stempel, den von dem eignen
blühenden Staub getroffnen, zur Scheinfrucht

44

The Fifth Elegy

TELL me who, who are these travellers, more fugitive, even,
than we? Who, from the very beginning, seem driven
and forced by a will – and whose is it? –
which unrelentingly wrings and bends them
hurls them and swings them; tosses them, catches them back?
... they descend through air that is slicker and smoother
on to the tattered old mat, on to the carpet
worn thin by their feet in that shuffling and leaping:
the mat lost somewhere in the cosmos –
stuck on like a plaster, as if
where suburbia's heaven had wounded the Earth.
   And, barely discernible, yet
there in its place and revealed, stands Destiny's
capital letter: its part to play skittles
with even the strongest – to roll them and bowl them,
relentlessly grasp them – as Augustus the Strong at his table
might twist a tin platter.

And around and about that focus,
the rose of the audience blossoms
... unpetals: and the pistil, that piston
caught by its own teeming pollen,
is once more tricked into

wieder der Unlust befruchteten, ihrer
niemals bewußten, – glänzend mit dünnster
Oberfläche leicht scheinlächelnden Unlust.

Da: der welke, faltige Stemmer,
der alte, der nur noch trommelt,
eingegangen in seiner gewaltigen Haut, als hätte sie früher
zwei Männer enthalten, und einer
läge nun schon auf dem Kirchhof, und er überlebte den andern,   30
taub und manchmal ein wenig
wirr, in der verwitweten Haut.

Aber der junge, der Mann, als wär er der Sohn eines Nackens
und einer Nonne: prall und strammig erfüllt
mit Muskeln und Einfalt.

O ihr,
die ein Leid, das noch klein war,
einst als Spielzeug bekam, in einer seiner
langen Genesungen...

Du, der mit dem Aufschlag,   40
wie nur Früchte ihn kennen, unreif
täglich hundert Mal abfällt vom Baum der gemeinsam
erbauten Bewegung, (der, rascher als Wasser, in wenig
Minuten Lenz, Sommer und Herbst hat) –
abfällt und anprallt ans Grab:
manchmal, in halber Pause, will dir ein liebes
Antlitz entstehn hinüber zu deiner selten
zärtlichen Mutter; doch an deinen Körper verliert sich,
der es flächig verbraucht, das schüchtern
kaum versuchte Gesicht...Und wieder   50
klatscht der Mann in die Hand zu dem Ansprung, und eh dir
jemals ein Schmerz deutlicher wird in der Nähe des immer
trabenden Herzens, kommt das Brennen der Fußsohln
ihm, seinem Ursprung, zuvor mit ein paar dir
rasch in die Augen gejagten leiblichen Tränen.
Und dennoch, blindlings,
das Lächeln...

Engel! o nimms, pflücks, das kleinblütige Heilkraut.
Schaff eine Vase, verwahrs! Stells unter jene, uns *noch* nicht

fool's-gold fertility...
the thin surface glitter,
the insincere, ignorant grin of satiety.

There stands the Weightlifter, now just a drummer,
wrinkled and withered and old, looking lost
inside the huge skin that, but lately,
might have cased two men: as if one of those two
were by now in his coffin, and he –
the inheritor – deaf and sometimes befuddled
lived on in that half-widowed skin.

But then there's the young man, the one
sired by a neck on a nun – all strapping and smartly-compounded
of muscle and mindlessness.

O you people, once given to Grief
for a plaything: still young, still
in the course of its own weary mending.

Then you: falling a hundred times daily
and bruising (still green!) from the tree
grown of everyone moving together (the tree
which swifter than water races its seasons;
into mere minutes crams Spring-Summer-Autumn)
... You land on the grave like a windfallen apple.
At intervals sometimes, a tender expression tries
to steal into your face – a glance for your mother
(herself rarely tender); but that barely sketched, fugitive look
passes from face into figure and finishes there.
    Here it comes:
here's the chap clapping hands for... The... Pyramid!
And before any pain can grow keener,
or nearer your galloping heart, he feels
that foot-tingling reminder of all that he springs from,
feels the quickening tears leap into his eyes
and nevertheless... blindly... the smile...!

Angel! O pluck that herb with its small blossoms
and fetch a vase for it, safeguard it well. Set it
among those other treasures we must wait for

offenen Freuden; in lieblicher Urne   60
rühms mit blumiger, schwungiger Aufschrift: *„Subrisio Saltat."*.
  Du dann, Liebliche,
du, von den reizendsten Freuden
stumm Übersprungne. Vielleicht sind
deine Fransen glücklich für dich – ,
oder über den jungen
prallen Brüsten die grüne metallene Seide
fühlt sich unendlich verwöhnt und entbehrt nichts.
Du, auf alle des Gleichgewichts schwankende Waagen
immerfort anders   70
hingelegte Marktfrucht des Gleichmuts,
öffentlich unter den Schultern.

Wo, o *wo* ist der Ort, – ich trag ihn im Herzen – ,
wo sie noch lange nicht *konnten*, noch von einander
abfieln, wie sich bespringende, nicht recht
paarige Tiere; –
wo die Gewichte noch schwer sind;
wo noch von ihren vergeblich
wirbelnden Stäben die Teller
torkeln...   80

Und plötzlich in diesem mühsamen Nirgends, plötzlich
die unsägliche Stelle, wo sich das reine Zuwenig
unbegreiflich verwandelt – , umspringt
in jenes leere Zuviel.
Wo die vielstellige Rechnung
zahlenlos aufgeht.

Plätze, o Platz in Paris, unendlicher Schauplatz,
wo die Modistin, *Madame Lamort*,
die ruhlosen Wege der Erde, endlose Bänder,
schlingt und windet und neue aus ihnen   90
Schleifen erfindet, Rüschen, Blumen, Kokarden, künstliche
                Früchte – , alle
unwahr gefärbt, – für die billigen
Winterhüte des Schicksals.
. . . .

and do it honour with a precious jar, and with
the florid, bold inscription: *Subrisio Saltat.*

You then, my lovely?
Over your head the most rousing pleasures
pass silently by. Perhaps all those flounces –
do they feel happiness for you? Or that silk –
greenly gleaming upon breasts still firm and still young –
thinks itself spoiled to distraction
and knows it lacks nothing.
You, child –
never the same for a moment, different in all
of the seesawing scales that would weigh you;
passive as produce, displayed on the stalls
among shouldering people.

Oh, where is it, where is it now: that time and that place
in my heart? The time before they'd grown confident,
practised and able; still came unstuck
from each other – like creatures mismated?
When the weights were still weighty;
when the plates of the jugglers still staggered off
and away from the tips
of the spin-sticks still foolishly twirling...

In this limbo of labour all of a sudden
the strange unpredictable point
where the starkly too-little bafflingly, suddenly, changes
place with the sham, with the glut of too-much;
where the sum with its too-many figures
leaves no remainder at all.

Paris. That permanent showplace:
Les Places; the place of the milliner, Madame Lamort,
working at fluttering ribbons of worldliness
stitching and twisting – endlessly fiddling
new bows and cockades, gewgaws, flowers,
fruits artificial in aniline colours...all
to adorn Fate's cheap winter hats.
. . . .

49

Engel: es wäre ein Platz, den wir nicht wissen, und dorten,
auf unsäglichem Teppich, zeigten die Liebenden, die's hier
bis zum Können nie bringen, ihre kühnen
hohen Figuren des Herzschwungs,
ihre Türme aus Lust, ihre
längst, wo Boden nie war, nur aneinander
lehnenden Leitern, bebend, – und *könntens*,   100
vor den Zuschauern rings, unzähligen lautlosen Toten:
Würfen die dann ihre letzten, immer ersparten,
immer verborgenen, die wir nicht kennen, ewig
gültigen Münzen des Glücks vor das endlich
wahrhaft lächelnde Paar auf gestilltem
Teppich?

Angel: suppose there were a place that we know nothing of,
and that in it lovers
– who never did find their fulfilment here below –
performed their showy, daring acts upon
the heart's trapeze, and built their towers of pleasure
from ladders each propped only by the other's
and standing, ever-swaying, where no ground is.
And suppose they found it;
suppose they found it with an audience around them
of the un-numberable and silent dead:
would not those dead then scatter
their last, their carefully-hoarded ever-kept-secret
coins of happiness – eternal legal tender –
before that couple who at last
are truthfully smiling, upon that ineffable carpet
. . . finally stilled?

Die sechste Elegie

FEIGENBAUM, seit wie lange schon ists mir bedeutend,
wie du die Blüte beinah ganz überschlägst
und hinein in die zeitig entschlossene Frucht,
ungerühmt, drängst dein reines Geheimnis.
Wie der Fontäne Rohr treibt dein gebognes Gezweig
abwärts den Saft und hinan: und es springt aus dem Schlaf,
fast nicht erwachend, ins Glück seiner süßesten Leistung.
Sieh: wie der Gott in den Schwan.
                                    ... Wir aber verweilen,
ach, uns rühmt es zu blühn, und ins verspätete Innre
unserer endlichen Frucht gehn wir verraten hinein.   10
Wenigen steigt so stark der Andrang des Handelns,
daß sie schon anstehn und glühn in der Fülle des Herzens,
wenn die Verführung zum Blühn wie gelinderte Nachtluft
ihnen die Jugend des Munds, ihnen die Lider berührt:
Helden vielleicht und den frühe Hinüberbestimmten,
denen der gärtnernde Tod anders die Adern verbiegt.
Diese stürzen dahin: dem eigenen Lächeln
sind sie voran, wie das Rossegespann in den milden
muldigen Bildern von Karnak dem siegenden König.

The Sixth Elegy

FIG Tree! When did I first truly notice
how, almost, you forbear to flower...
how modestly you pack away your secret
inside those early-determined fruits...?
Arching, your branches pump the sap downwards, then up
as through the pipes of a fountain; scarcely awaking
it springs straight from sleep, gladly to offer
the sweetest of harvests...See: the God enters the Swan!
    Yet, for our own part we linger...flowering flatters us...
betrayed by that flowering, we enter at last
our own fruit, so long delayed in its ripening.
Few there are that the challenge of action can kindle
so that – at once – they stand ready
and glow in their fullness of heart! Heroes, perhaps,
and those others predestined for earliest reaping,
for whom Death, the Head Gardener, has laid
strange paths for their life's-blood to run in.
Who, when the thrill, the seduction of flowering
steals on them and touches the lips of the young, breathes
on their eyelids like night's gentle air...who,
rushing in headlong, outstrip their own smiling faces;
as, in the low-relief panels at Karnac, the chariot-
team pulls away in the van of the conquering king...

Wunderlich nah ist der Held doch den jugendlich Toten. Dauern   20
ficht ihn nicht an. Sein Aufgang ist Dasein; beständig
nimmt er sich fort und tritt ins veränderte Sternbild
seiner steten Gefahr. Dort fänden ihn wenige. Aber,
das uns finster verschweigt, das plötzlich begeisterte Schicksal
singt ihn hinein in den Sturm seiner aufrauschenden Welt.
Hör ich doch keinen wie *ihn*. Auf einmal durchgeht mich
mit der strömenden Luft sein verdunkelter Ton.

Dann, wie verbärg ich mich gern vor der Sehnsucht: O wär ich,
wär ich ein Knabe und dürft es noch werden und säße
in die künftigen Arme gestützt und läse von Simson,   30
wie seine Mutter erst nichts und dann alles gebar.

War er nicht Held schon in dir, o Mutter, begann nicht
dort schon, in dir, seine herrische Auswahl?
Tausende brauten im Schooß und wollten *er* sein,
aber sieh: er ergriff und ließ aus, wählte und konnte.
Und wenn er Säulen zerstieß, so wars, da er ausbrach
aus der Welt deines Leibs in die engere Welt, wo er weiter
wählte und konnte. O Mütter der Helden,
o Ursprung reißender Ströme! Ihr Schluchten, in die sich
hoch von dem Herzrand, klagend,   40
schon die Mädchen gestürzt, künftig die Opfer dem Sohn.

Denn hinstürmte der Held durch Aufenthalte der Liebe,
jeder hob ihn hinaus, jeder ihn meinende Herzschlag,
abgewendet schon, stand er am Ende der Lächeln, – anders.

The Hero – and those who die young:
so strangely and closely related!
Permanence doesn't concern him: he *is there*
from his very beginning. Yet he ever sets forth
for changed constellations of unchanging danger.
Few there are who would find him there. Yet Fate –
so forbidding and dumb to us others –
Fate, all of a sudden enraptured –
sings him into the storms of his turbulent world.
I hear none who is like him: all at once
his shadowy cry, borne on the wind, pierces me!

Then, how willing I'd be to find it, the place
where I might hide from yearning;
oh, if I were yet a mere lad,
still in the midst of becoming,
I could sit propped in the arms of the future
and read stories of Samson, of him
whose mother bore nothing at first. Yet later bore all.

Was he not ever the Hero – within you, his mother?
Was it not made inside you, his first own imperious choice?
Of those thousands that swarmed in the womb
and that willed to become him?
Yet, see! how he takes up, lets fall; chooses, is able to *do* it.
Now he's Destroyer of Columns. Even now
he's the same; sprung from the world of your body
and out into narrowing World
he continues to choose; and continues
able to *act*. O Mothers of Heroes! O you wellsprings
of white-water torrents! O you chasms, from whose tall heart-edge
have leaped the sorrowing maidens destined
for sacrifice to the son!

For the Hero . . . storms headlong through Love's halting-places,
each heartbeat for him urges him further, past them,
                    beyond them . . .
he breaks through to the end of the Smiles: grown other.

Die siebente Elegie

WERBUNG nicht mehr, nicht Werbung, entwachsene Stimme,
sei deines Schreies Natur; zwar schrieest du rein wie der Vogel,
wenn ihn die Jahreszeit aufhebt, die steigende, beinah vergessend,
daß er ein kümmerndes Tier und nicht nur ein einzelnes Herz sei,
das sie ins Heitere wirft, in die innigen Himmel. Wie er, so
würbest du wohl, nicht minder –, daß, noch unsichtbar,
dich die Freundin erführ, die stille, in der eine Antwort
langsam erwacht und über dem Hören sich anwärmt, –
deinem erkühnten Gefühl die erglühte Gefühlin.

O und der Frühling begriffe –, da ist keine Stelle,   10
die nicht trüge den Ton Verkündigung. Erst jenen kleinen
fragenden Auflaut, den mit steigernder Stille
weithin umschweigt ein reiner, bejahender Tag.
Dann die Stufen hinan, Ruf-Stufen hinan, zum geträumten
Tempel der Zukunft –; dann den Triller, Fontäne,
die zu dem drängenden Strahl schon das Fallen zuvornimmt
im versprechlichen Spiel... Und vor sich, den Sommer.
Nicht nur die Morgen alle des Sommers –, nicht nur
wie sie sich wandeln in Tag und strahlen vor Anfang.

The Seventh Elegy

No more of your courtship! an end to all wooing,
    o tongue that's outgrown it!
Let that be the sense of your cry. And if you cried
as piercing as ever bird sang, exulting
in surging of season, forgetting he's only an unquiet creature
and thinking himself soul at its purest – chosen uniquely
for springtime to fling into heights of gladness,
into highest Heaven.
You too have your talent for wooing: hidden as yet –
but sending out signals to beckon a mistress, who,
passive at first, soon kindles in listening to love –
finding a glow to answer the warmth of her lover!

To the Spring, none of this is a secret:
not one place, not one corner, immune to the mood
                of annunciation.
All affirmation, the mood of the halcyon day mutely
answers that small questioning voice; answers with stillness
steadily deepening... extending. Then, up the steps, song-steps;
stairway that mounts to the dream of the Temple of Future.
The trill: fountain whose falling jet races
and teases its rising... playfully changing to spray.
And Summer lies waiting.
                Not just all Summer dawns...
not just their turning to day (that light before first light).

57

Nicht nur die Tage, die zart sind um Blumen, und oben,   20
um die gestalteten Bäume, stark und gewaltig.
Nicht nur die Andacht dieser entfalteten Kräfte,
nicht nur die Wege, nicht nur die Wiesen im Abend,
nicht nur, nach spätem Gewitter, das atmende Klarsein,
nicht nur der nahende Schlaf und ein Ahnen, abends...
sondern die Nächte! Sondern die hohen, des Sommers,
Nächte, sondern die Sterne, die Sterne der Erde.
O einst tot sein und sie wissen unendlich,
alle die Sterne: denn wie, wie, wie sie vergessen!

Siehe, da rief ich die Liebende. Aber nicht *sie* nur   30
käme... Es kämen aus schwächlichen Gräbern
Mädchen und ständen... Denn, wie beschränk ich,
wie, den gerufenen Ruf? Die Versunkenen suchen
immer noch Erde. – Ihr Kinder, ein hiesig
einmal ergriffenes Ding gälte für viele.
Glaubt nicht, Schicksal sei mehr als das Dichte der Kindheit;
wie überholtet ihr oft den Geliebten, atmend,
atmend nach seligem Lauf, auf nichts zu, ins Freie.

Hiersein ist herrlich. Ihr wußtet es, Mädchen, *ihr* auch,
die ihr scheinbar entbehrtet, versankt –, ihr, in den ärgsten   40
Gassen der Städte, Schwärende, oder dem Abfall
offene. Denn eine Stunde war jeder, vielleicht nicht
ganz eine Stunde, ein mit den Maßen der Zeit kaum
Meßliches zwischen zwei Weilen –, da sie ein Dasein
hatte. Alles. Die Adern voll Dasein.
Nur, wir vergessen so leicht, was der lachende Nachbar
uns nicht bestätigt oder beneidet. Sichtbar
wollen wirs heben, wo doch das sichtbarste Glück uns
erst zu erkennen sich gibt, wenn wir es innen verwandeln.

Nirgends, Geliebte, wird Welt sein, als innen. Unser   50
Leben geht hin mit Verwandlung. Und immer geringer
schwindet das Außen. Wo einmal ein dauerndes Haus war,
schlägt sich erdachtes Gebild vor, quer, zu Erdenklichem

Not only tender days which lie soft about flowers
(with above them the trees, sculptured, mighty and stark).
Not only the loving devotion revealed by those Powers;
not only the paths, not only meadows at twilight,
not that breathing at dusk, not that brightness which follows
           the storm;
not only, when sleep draws near of an evening,
the foretaste of knowledge just dawning...
but the nights, but the nights too, those tall nights
of Summer; but the stars too, the stars of our Earth.
Oh! to lie dead at last; know them eternal;
all the stars; how could they – how could *those* be forgotten?

What if I called out for her, for my mistress?
...Why, others might answer. All those frail graves
might deliver up girls who would answer and stand;
how could one limit the cry that was cried...?
for the Drowned must endlessly search for dry land.
You children: one single thing
truly experienced in the here and now
might stand token for many things. Never believe that Destiny
means more than your sense-laden childhood.
    Have you not often outdistanced your lover
breathlessly...happily...running, heading for nowhere at all?
Being is marvellous! You knew it, even you girls who were losers
– dragged down in the slum-alleys of cities:
festering there, exposed to all rottenness. For each
had her hour of being: blood running full with it –
all of it *hers*! But, not an hour exactly,
only the span between one time and another,
not to be measured in measures of time.
...Yet we are quick to forget all that the smiling
faces-next-door do not echo or covet.
If we can see it we praise it, ever forgetting
how the joy that's most visible passes us by
...isn't ours till we grasp and transform it; inside us.

Beloved: World has no place
if not some place within us. Our own lives
pass in transformation. All that's around us – outside us –
continually passes, endlessly dwindles. Where a house
used to stand as if it were permanent, a sheer concept,

völlig gehörig, als ständ es noch ganz im Gehirne.
Weite Speicher der Kraft schafft sich der Zeitgeist, gestaltlos
wie der spannende Drang, den er aus allem gewinnt.
Tempel kennt er nicht mehr. Diese, des Herzens, Verschwendung
sparen wir heimlicher ein. Ja, wo noch eins übersteht,
ein einst gebetetes Ding, ein gedientes, geknietes –,
hält es sich, so wie es ist, schon ins Unsichtbare hin.   60
Viele gewahrens nicht mehr, doch ohne den Vorteil,
daß sie's nun *innerlich* baun, mit Pfeilern und Statuen, größer!

Jede dumpfe Umkehr der Welt hat solche Enterbte,
denen das Frühere nicht und noch nicht das Nächste gehört.
Denn auch das Nächste ist weit für die Menschen. *Uns* soll
dies nicht verwirren; es stärke in uns die Bewahrung
der noch erkannten Gestalt. Dies *stand* einmal unter Menschen,
mitten im Schicksal stands, im vernichtenden, mitten
im Nichtwissen-Wohin stand es, wie seiend, und bog
Sterne zu sich aus gesicherten Himmeln. Engel,   70
dir noch zeig ich es, *da*! in deinem Anschaun
steh es gerettet zuletzt, nun endlich aufrecht.
Säulen, Pylone, der Sphinx, das strebende Stemmen,
grau aus vergehender Stadt oder aus fremder, des Doms.

War es nicht Wunder? O staune, Engel, denn *wir* sinds,
wir, o du Großer, erzähls, daß wir solches vermochten, mein Atem
reicht für die Rühmung nicht aus. So haben wir dennoch
nicht die Räume versäumt, diese gewährenden, diese,
unsere Räume. (Was müssen sie fürchterlich groß sein,
da sie Jahrtausende nicht unseres Fühlns überfülln.)   80
Aber ein Turm war groß, nicht wahr? O Engel, er war es, –
groß, auch noch neben dir? Chartres war groß – und Musik
reichte noch weiter hinan und überstieg uns. Doch selbst nur

structured and rational, takes over; to stand in the mind
as some brain's pure invention.
Giant silos of power are born of the *Zeitgeist*;
charged by potentials wrung from and active in all.
Places of worship are no longer known to it;
such things – expenses of spirit, extravagant –
we who are Modern are learning to hoard.
Some things remain, and those survivals, the very things
once most prayed to, attended and bowed to –
stay just as they are and survive, out of sight.
Many no longer know them, and forfeit the richer rewards
of building *within*, with effigies, columns, temples far greater!

Every sad turn-about of our World possesses
those self-dispossessed of inheritance,
those without past to whom no future belongs.
For, from ourselves, even what's closest lies distant…
but that need not confuse us, should rather encourage
to keep and preserve in ourselves the imprint of all
that once was…and was known…and has passed.
Once this was a knowledge which stood
revealed amongst all men; stood through all Destiny; withstood
all chaos. Through every grim loss of direction…it *stood*
as something that *is*, and that plucks from the safety of Heaven
and to its own will bends the stars! Angel: I'll show you:
there! let it stand. Finally saved, yes, in *your* vision
established at last: columns and pylons and Sphinx;
thrusting up greyly and rising:
leaving our city, or where we are strangers:
cathedral and spire.

Who could believe it? Oh, marvel, Angel:
Angel, oh, tell it…It was we, we ourselves
who were capable of it! My own breath will not serve to extol it.
So, in the end, we have not failed this space of ours –
these generous spaces (frighteningly vast; thousands of years;
still the sum of our feelings does not overflow it).
And…greatness?
– One *tower*, surely, was great. Angel; it was.
– Great, even by *your* side?
– Chartres was great. And *music* reached higher,
transcending its makers. Even a woman in love,

61

eine Liebende, oh, allein am nächtlichen Fenster...
reichte sie dir nicht ans Knie –?

                       Glaub *nicht*, daß ich werbe.
Engel, und würb ich dich auch! Du kommst nicht. Denn mein
Anruf ist immer voll Hinweg; wider so starke
Strömung kannst du nicht schreiten. Wie ein gestreckter
Arm ist mein Rufen. Und seine zum Greifen
oben offene Hand bleibt vor dir   90
offen, wie Abwehr und Warnung,
Unfaßlicher, weitauf.

alone by her window at night –
would she not measure, at least, to your knee?
Angel, do not mistake this for wooing,
for, if I did woo – would that bring you near?
The cry that I cry out to you
has the press of a current; you cannot make way
against so strong a tide. Like an arm outstretched
is my calling...Its hand, raised and open
and ready to grasp, stays open before you...
holding off: giving warning
to you: the Ungraspable.

Die achte Elegie

Rudolf Kaßner zugeeignet

MIT allen Augen sieht die Kreatur
das Offene. Nur unsre Augen sind
wie umgekehrt und ganz um sie gestellt
als Fallen, rings um ihren freien Ausgang.
Was draußen *ist*, wir wissens aus des Tiers
Antlitz allein; denn schon das frühe Kind
wenden wir um und zwingens, daß es rückwärts
Gestaltung sehe, nicht das Offne, das
im Tiergesicht so tief ist. Frei von Tod.
Ihn sehen wir allein; das freie Tier   10
hat seinen Untergang stets hinter sich
und vor sich Gott, und wenn es geht, so gehts
in Ewigkeit, so wie die Brunnen gehen.
    Wir haben nie, nicht einen einzigen Tag,
den reinen Raum vor uns, in den die Blumen
unendlich aufgehn. Immer ist es Welt
und niemals Nirgends ohne Nicht: das Reine,
Unüberwachte, das man atmet und
unendlich *weiß* und nicht begehrt. Als Kind
verliert sich eins im Stilln an dies und wird   20
gerüttelt. Oder jener stirbt und ists.
Denn nah am Tod sieht man den Tod nicht mehr

The Eighth Elegy

ALL eyes, the creatures of the World look out
into the open. But our human eyes,
as if turned right around and glaring in,
encircle them; prohibiting their passing.
What lies outside, their faces plainly show us.
Yet we compel even our youngest; force
each child always to stare behind, at what's
already manifest, and not to see
that openness which lies so deep within
the gaze of animals. Death leaves beasts free.
Only we foreknow it. Animals
keep death behind them, and before them, God.
And when a beast passes, it passes in
eternity, as rivers run...
    We never have, not for a single day,
pure *space* before us – all its flowers
opening endlessly: there is ever World.
We never find that nowhere, free from
negatives, unsupervised and pure; the place
which we might breathe and know unendingly,
and never crave. While we stay children, we
can get lost in that stillness – till something
jogs us from it. Or we may die: become it.
For, close to dying, we need see death no more

und starrt *hinaus*, vielleicht mit großem Tierblick.
Liebende, wäre nicht der andre, der
die Sicht verstellt, sind nah daran und staunen...
Wie aus Versehn ist ihnen aufgetan
hinter dem andern... Aber über ihn
kommt keiner fort, und wieder wird ihm Welt.
Der Schöpfung immer zugewendet, sehn
wir nur auf ihr die Spiegelung des Frein,   30
von uns verdunkelt. Oder daß ein Tier,
ein stummes, aufschaut, ruhig durch uns durch.
Dieses heißt Schicksal: gegenüber sein
und nichts als das und immer gegenüber.

Wäre Bewußtheit unsrer Art in dem
sicheren Tier, das uns entgegenzieht
in anderer Richtung –, riß es uns herum
mit seinem Wandel. Doch sein Sein ist ihm
unendlich, ungefaßt und ohne Blick
auf seinen Zustand, rein, so wie sein Ausblick.   40
Und wo wir Zukunft sehn, dort sieht es alles
und sich in allem und geheilt für immer.

Und doch ist in dem wachsam warmen Tier
Gewicht und Sorge einer großen Schwermut.
Denn ihm auch haftet immer an, was uns
oft überwältigt, – die Erinnerung,
als sei schon einmal das, wonach man drängt,
näher gewesen, treuer und sein Anschluß
unendlich zärtlich. Hier ist alles Abstand,
und dort wars Atem. Nach der ersten Heimat   50
ist ihm die zweite zwitterig und windig.
    O Seligkeit der *kleinen* Kreatur,
die immer *bleibt* im Schooße, der sie austrug;
o Glück der Mücke, die noch *innen* hüpft,
selbst wenn sie Hochzeit hat: denn Schooß ist alles.
Und sieh die halbe Sicherheit des Vogels,
der beinah beides weiß aus seinem Ursprung,
als wär er eine Seele der Etrusker,
aus einem Toten, den ein Raum empfing,

and can, perhaps, look outwards with a gaze
as wide as is the gaze of animals.
Lovers, were it not for that other one
whose presence blocks their sight, might come to it,
amazed. As if by chance, they catch a glimpse –
half-hidden by each other. Yet they still
cannot see past that other: all too soon
the World has hold of them again.
 Our gaze is ever turned towards Creation;
we know only the surface of that glass,
its clouded image, by our selves obscured.
And yet, sometimes a silent animal
looks up at us and silently looks through us.
We call it Fate to be in opposition.
Nothing but that. Forever opposite.

If they possessed our kind of consciousness
those steady animals, whose own direction
always counters ours, would wrench us around
to follow where they lead. To animals
their being is infinite, unknowable;
and they look *out* from it, not at themselves.
And where we see future, they see the whole;
themselves within it; held and healed forever.
 Yet, watchful and warmblooded as they are,
those animals know all the weight, the sadness,
of a heavy heart. For, just like us,
they are the prey of memory...as if all
we strive for now had, once upon a time,
been closer and more intimately ours:
more faithful to us. As if all things now
abandoned us – which once lived close as breath.
To any who have known a better World,
our own feels windswept and ambivalent.
 How happy are those tiny creatures who
continue in the womb which gave them life.
Happy the gnat: even its nuptial dance
is danced within the womb. Womb is all things.
Look at the birds, at their half-certainty,
who seem to fly with one wing in each world
as if they were the souls escaping from
Etruscan dead...from one who shares a box

doch mit der ruhenden Figur als Deckel. 60
Und wie bestürzt ist eins, das fliegen muß
und stammt aus einem Schooß. Wie vor sich selbst
erschreckt, durchzuckts die Luft, wie wenn ein Sprung
durch eine Tasse geht. So reißt die Spur
der Fledermaus durchs Porzellan des Abends.

Und wir: Zuschauer, immer, überall,
dem allen zugewandt und nie hinaus!
Uns überfüllts. Wir ordnens. Es zerfällt.
Wir ordnens wieder und zerfallen selbst.

Wer hat uns also umgedreht, daß wir, 70
was wir auch tun, in jener Haltung sind
von einem, welcher fortgeht? Wie er auf
dem letzten Hügel, der ihm ganz sein Tal
noch einmal zeigt, sich wendet, anhält, weilt –,
so leben wir und nehmen immer Abschied.

with his own effigy, at liberty,
reposing on the lid. And how perplexed
must any womb-born creature feel, who is
obliged to fly thin air. As if in panic
fear they flitter through that sky... afraid
of flight itself: swift as a flaw runs through
a cup, the lightning passage of a bat
makes hair-cracks in the porcelain of dusk.

And we, we stay spectators; turned towards
all things and still transcending none.
All overwhelms us. We set all in order.
All falls apart. We order it once more
and fall, collapse, disintegrate ourselves.

How were we first persuaded to perform
our every act as though it were our last?
As one might halt upon the last high ground,
which shows him his own valley one last time,
and turn; and linger; and hang back...
... so we dwell here, forever taking leave.

Die neunte Elegie

WARUM, wenn es angeht, also die Frist des Daseins
hinzubringen, als Lorbeer, ein wenig dunkler als alles
andere Grün, mit kleinen Wellen an jedem
Blattrand (wie eines Windes Lächeln) – : warum dann
Menschliches müssen – und, Schicksal vermeidend,
sich sehnen nach Schicksal?...

                 O, *nicht*, weil Glück *ist*,
dieser voreilige Vorteil eines nahen Verlusts.
Nicht aus Neugier, oder zur Übung des Herzens,
das auch im Lorbeer *wäre*...
Aber weil Hiersein viel ist, und weil uns scheinbar   10
alles das Hiesige braucht, dieses Schwindende, das
seltsam uns angeht. Uns, die Schwindendsten. *Ein* Mal
jedes, nur *ein* Mal. *Ein* Mal und nicht mehr. Und wir auch
ein Mal. Nie wieder. Aber dieses
ein Mal gewesen zu sein, wenn auch nur *ein* Mal:
irdisch gewesen zu sein, scheint nicht widerrufbar.

Und so drängen wir uns und wollen es leisten,
wollens enthalten in unsern einfachen Händen,

The Ninth Elegy

WHY, when it finally comes down to this, to living out
our own brief span of life...which, like the laurel,
wears its own green some few tones deeper
than all other greens around it, and bears the rippled edge
to every leaf that flutters like the smiling of a breeze...
why should we, marked down to live as mortals,
still yearn for Destiny even while we persist
in struggling to escape from Destiny?
...Oh, not for Fortune,
not for quick profit, soon overtaken by loss.
Not for curiosity. Neither to exercise any
heart which might beat within laurel...
but because living means much, and
because we ourselves seem to be needed
by all things present; by the here and the now;
by this fleeting World, for it touches us nearly;
touches us, the most fleeting, once only.
Only once for each and for all; once and no more.
Ourselves one time only and never again.
But to have lived for that once, even if only the one time
to have been human, been mortal, stands fast and seems
irrevocable.

So that, wanting to give Life its due, we urge ourselves on;
seeking to hold on to Life, to contain it

im überfüllteren Blick und im sprachlosen Herzen.
Wollen es werden. Wem es geben? Am liebsten   20
alles behalten für immer... Ach, in den andern Bezug,
wehe, was nimmt man hinüber? Nicht das Anschaun, das hier
langsam erlernte, und kein hier Ereignetes. Keins.
Also die Schmerzen. Also vor allem das Schwersein,
also der Liebe lange Erfahrung, – also
lauter Unsägliches. Aber später,
unter den Sternen, was solls: *die* sind *besser* unsäglich.
Bringt doch der Wanderer auch vom Hange des Bergrands
nicht eine Hand voll Erde ins Tal, die allen unsägliche, sondern
ein erworbenes Wort, reines, den gelben und blaun   30
Enzian. Sind wir vielleicht *hier*, um zu sagen: Haus,
Brücke, Brunnen, Tor, Krug, Obstbaum, Fenster, –
höchstens: Säule, Turm... aber zu *sagen*, verstehs,
o zu sagen *so*, wie selber die Dinge niemals
innig meinten zu sein. Ist nicht die heimliche List
dieser verschwiegenen Erde, wenn sie die Liebenden drängt,
daß sich in ihrem Gefühl jedes und jedes entzückt?
Schwelle: was ists für zwei
Liebende, daß sie die eigne ältere Schwelle der Tür
ein wenig verbrauchen, auch sie, nach den vielen vorher   40
und vor den künftigen..., leicht.

Hier ist des *Säglichen* Zeit, *hier* seine Heimat.
Sprich und bekenn. Mehr als je
fallen die Dinge dahin, die erlebbaren, denn,
was sie verdrängend ersetzt, ist ein Tun ohne Bild.
Tun unter Krusten, die willig zerspringen, sobald
innen das Handeln entwächst und sich anders begrenzt.

within our bare hands; through overstrained eyes to see it;
to speak it from dumb, inarticulate hearts.
We yearn to become it: to whom might we give it?
We ask nothing less than to hold Life forever.
But, alas! into that other dimension...
what can we take across with us?
Not sight: not our skill in seeing which, here,
we were so long in learning. Not any
among all the events which took place here. Not one.
So that leaves us our sorrows. It leaves us
before all else, sheer weight of life. Leaves the many
long-drawn encounters of love; leaves those many things
which are unsayable. And later then, under the stars?
What of them, they are better unsayable...!
For, even the traveller, come down from the heights,
brings down to the valley, no handful of earth –
for that would say nothing; he bears the sheer word
won from the gentian; its message of yellow, of blue.
Were we put in this World here, truly, for speech? To say:
House, Fountain, Bridge, Gate, Jug, Fruit Tree; or Window?
Or even rise higher and say the word: Column?
Say: Tower? But to say these, remember,
to speak them...in a manner that those things,
at heart, never intended to *be*? Could it be...
might not this be the World's cunning purpose,
speechlessly, secretly urging all lovers
so that each thing and all things themselves might
rejoice in the feelings they feel...?
Threshold: what might it mean to two lovers
to find themselves treading and wearing
a threshold – their own but much older;
following all who preceded; before those who follow...
...mean little?

Ours the Age of the Sayable. Ours its parish.
Speak and bear witness! More than ever before,
things once open for us to experience
are replaced, thrust aside by action that lacks any image;
action encrusted, yet ready to break from its shell –
when what's active within it outgrows it and seeks for new limits.

Zwischen den Hämmern besteht
unser Herz, wie die Zunge
zwischen den Zähnen, die doch,
dennoch die preisende bleibt.

Preise dem Engel die Welt, nicht die unsägliche, *ihm*
kannst du nicht großtun mit herrlich Erfühltem; im Weltall,
wo er fühlender fühlt, bist du ein Neuling. Drum zeig
ihm das Einfache, das, von Geschlecht zu Geschlechtern gestaltet,
als ein Unsriges lebt neben der Hand und im Blick.
Sag ihm die Dinge. Er wird staunender stehn; wie du standest
bei dem Seiler in Rom, oder beim Töpfer am Nil.
Zeig ihm, wie glücklich ein Ding sein kann, wie schuldlos und
                unser,
wie selbst das klagende Leid rein zur Gestalt sich entschließt,
dient als ein Ding, oder stirbt in ein Ding –, und jenseits
selig der Geige entgeht. Und diese, von Hingang
lebenden Dinge verstehn, daß du sie rühmst; vergänglich,
traun sie ein Rettendes uns, den Vergänglichsten, zu.
Wollen, wir sollen sie ganz im unsichtbarn Herzen verwandeln
in – o unendlich – in uns! wer wir am Ende auch seien.

Erde, ist es nicht dies, was du willst: *unsichtbar*
in uns erstehn? – Ist es dein Traum nicht,
einmal unsichtbar zu sein? – Erde! unsichtbar!
Was, wenn Verwandlung nicht, ist dein drängender Auftrag?
Erde, du liebe, ich will. O glaub, es bedürfte
nicht deiner Frühlinge mehr, mich dir zu gewinnen –, *einer*,
ach, ein einziger ist schon dem Blute zu viel.
Namenlos bin ich zu dir entschlossen, von weit her.
Immer warst du im Recht, und dein heiliger Einfall
ist der vertrauliche Tod.

Between hammer and hammer it dwells
and it beats, our own heart. As our tongue
lives between its own teeth,
and yet still continues in praise!

Praise this World to the Angel: not some world
transcendental, unsayable; you cannot impress him
with what is sublimely-experienced...
In this cosmos you are but recent and he
feels with more feeling...so, show him something
straightforward. Some simple thing fashioned
by one generation after another;
some object of ours – something
accustomed to living under our eyes and our hands.
Tell him *things*. He will stand in amazement, just as you
once stood by the Nile, watched the potters;
stood by the ropers in Rome, watched them at work.
Show him how happy a thing can be; innocent, faithful;
how even the crying of grief may chastely decide
to take on some manifest shape – and serve
as a thing; or die in a thing; or even –
pure and transcended – the violin singing!
And these things, whose own life is nourished by dying,
will hear how you praise and commend them, and, mortal,
entrust their survival to us, the most mortal of all;
willing us, wishing that we
in our hiddenest hearts might translate them
and take them – O World without end! – take them into
ourselves...whatever our selves may finally be.

Earth: is it not *this*, your desire? Invisibly...
within ourselves...to establish your being?
Is not your dream one day to stand here
invisible? Earth! No longer visible!
And, if not transformation, what have you set me as mission?
Earth, World that is dearest, I shall; oh, believe it!
Seasons of Spring are no longer needed,
every one of them richer than blood could endure,
to win me and keep me your own...
yours from the first: unnamed but already indentured.
You were never mistaken; Death, familiar and ours,
is your gift, was your sacred invention.

Siehe, ich lebe. Woraus? Weder Kindheit noch Zukunft
werden weniger...Überzähliges Dasein
entspringt mir im Herzen.

See, I am living! What lives me? Nor childhood, nor future
diminish. Surpassing all number,
sheer *being* leaps in my heart.

Die zehnte Elegie

DASS ich dereinst, an dem Ausgang der grimmigen Einsicht,
Jubel und Ruhm aufsinge zustimmenden Engeln.
Daß von den klargeschlagenen Hämmern des Herzens
keiner versage an weichen, zweifelnden oder
reißenden Saiten. Daß mich mein strömendes Antlitz
glänzender mache: daß das unscheinbare Weinen
blühe. O wie werdet ihr dann, Nächte, mir lieb sein,
gehärmte. Daß ich euch knieender nicht, untröstliche Schwestern,
hinnahm, nicht in euer gelöstes
Haar mich gelöster ergab. Wir, Vergeuder der Schmerzen.   10
Wie wir sie absehn voraus, in die traurige Dauer,
ob sie nicht enden vielleicht. Sie aber sind ja
unser winterwähriges Laub, unser dunkeles Sinngrün,
eine der Zeiten des heimlichen Jahres –, nicht nur
Zeit –, sind Stelle, Siedelung, Lager, Boden, Wohnort.

Freilich, wehe, wie fremd sind die Gassen der Leid-Stadt,
wo in der falschen, aus Übertönung gemachten
Stille, stark, aus der Gußform des Leeren der Ausguß,
prahlt: der vergoldete Lärm, das platzende Denkmal.
O, wie spurlos zerträte ein Engel ihnen den Trostmarkt,   20

The Tenth Elegy

WOULD that, emerging from depths of the bitterest insight,
one day I might lift up my voice and sing
to the chorusing Angels in loud affirmation!
Would that the truly-struck hammers of heart
sound never on strings loosened, weakened or torn!
May the tears that I shed make me shine brighter;
may those unshed then secretly flower –
oh, how I would cherish you then, nights of grieving!
Oh, Sisters of Grief that is Endless, I should have bowed lower
and knelt to receive you – I should have lost
myself in the flow of your free-flowing hair.
We are spendthrifts of sorrows, discount them too early,
trusting that even the longest must end.
                                        For they
are our tree dressed for its Winter, a darker mood-green;
one season out of our own private year. Sorrow is both
season and place; settlement, site, encampment and dwelling.

Distant and foreign to us, the streets of the City of Mourning,
in their silence noise-deafened and false. False, too,
those effigies; smug and self-preening, cast from the sandmoulds
                of emptiness;
hollow of purpose, begilded, bombastic! Oh, how completely
                an Angel
might trample such trading in sham consolation,

den die Kirche begrenzt, ihre fertig gekaufte:
reinlich und zu und enttäuscht wie ein Postamt am Sonntag.
Draußen aber kräuseln sich immer die Ränder von Jahrmarkt.
Schaukeln der Freiheit! Taucher und Gaukler des Eifers!
Und des behübschten Glücks figürliche Schießstatt,
wo es zappelt von Ziel und sich blechern benimmt,
wenn ein Geschickterer trifft. Von Beifall zu Zufall
taumelt er weiter; denn Buden jeglicher Neugier
werben, trommeln und plärrn. Für Erwachsene aber
ist noch besonders zu sehn, wie das Geld sich vermehrt,
                anatomisch, 30
nicht zur Belustigung nur: der Geschlechtsteil des Gelds,
alles, das Ganze, der Vorgang –, das unterrichtet und macht
fruchtbar...
...O aber gleich darüber hinaus,
hinter der letzten Planke, beklebt mit Plakaten des „Todlos",
jenes bitteren Biers, das den Trinkenden süß scheint,
wenn sie immer dazu frische Zerstreuungen kaun...,
gleich im Rücken der Planke, gleich dahinter, ists *wirklich*.
Kinder spielen, und Liebende halten einander abseits,
ernst, im ärmlichen Gras, und Hunde haben Natur.
Weiter noch zieht es den Jüngling; vielleicht, daß er eine junge 40
Klage liebt...Hinter ihr her kommt er in Wiesen. Sie sagt:
Weit. Wir wohnen dort draußen...Wo? Und der Jüngling
folgt. Ihn rührt ihre Haltung. Die Schulter, der Hals –, vielleicht
ist sie von herrlicher Herkunft. Aber er läßt sie, kehrt um,
wendet sich, winkt...Was solls? Sie ist eine Klage.

Nur die jungen Toten, im ersten Zustand
zeitlosen Gleichmuts, dem der Entwöhnung,
folgen ihr liebend. Mädchen
wartet sie ab und befreundet sie. Zeigt ihnen leise,
was sie an sich hat. Perlen des Leids und die feinen 50
Schleier der Duldung. – Mit Jünglingen geht sie
schweigend.

all those readymade comforts dispensed by the Church
(tidy, frustrated and shut as the Post on a Sunday).
Meanwhile... all the time milling and throbbing around it,
the fairground; the Fair! Freedom! The swings and the roundabouts;
tumblers and jugglers – personified zeal!
Shooting booths... where you aim at prettified puppets
that figure for Fortune, that fidget and jerk out of line
and tumble like tins when the marksman outwits them
...he then stumbles on, staggering
from good luck to pot-luck, to booths which promise him
every diversion, soliciting, beckoning, drumming him in!
But, something especially worth seeing is marked:

>*Adults Only!*
>*The Sex Life of Money. Full Anatomic Description.*
>*Full Details.*

More than a mere entertainment – How Money multiplies:
Its generative organs: Money in mating, at foreplay:
Instructive, amazing, arousing!
    ...Just opposite, only just after
the last of the hoardings (plastered with posters for Deathless,
that bitterest beer which tastes sweet – if you remember
to buy some Distractions to chew as you drink)
here things are real!...
Children are playing, and lovers, a little apart,
hold one another on thin, threadbare grass;
and dogs will be dogs.
The young man, lovesick, perhaps, for a girl, for a Grief
...follows through meadows, behind her. Far away, she tells him:
We live far away – over there.
                         Where? And still the youth follows her,
moved by something about her. Her neck. Those shoulders.
Her bearing... is she of noble descent?
But he finally leaves her. He waves and turns back:
after all, she is only Grief.

Only the young Dead – still learning their timeless serenity,
still being weaned – follow her lovingly.
                         And she
waits for the maidens, befriends them, quietly shows
what she is wearing. Pearls of Hurt. The delicate
Veils of Endurance. When she walks with young men
        she stays silent.

81

Aber dort, wo sie wohnen, im Tal, der älteren eine, der Klagen,
nimmt sich des Jünglings an, wenn er fragt: – Wir waren,
sagt sie, ein großes Geschlecht, einmal, wir Klagen. Die Väter
trieben den Bergbau dort in dem großen Gebirg; bei Menschen
findest du manchmal ein Stück geschliffenes Urleid
oder, aus altem Vulkan, schlackig versteinerten Zorn.
Ja, das stammte von dort. Einst waren wir reich. –

Und sie leitet ihn leicht durch die weite Landschaft der Klagen,   60
zeigt ihm die Säulen der Tempel oder die Trümmer
jener Burgen, von wo Klage-Fürsten das Land
einstens weise beherrscht. Zeigt ihm die hohen
Tränenbäume und Felder blühender Wehmut,
(Lebendige kennen sie nur als sanftes Blattwerk);
zeigt ihm die Tiere der Trauer, weidend, – und manchmal
schreckt ein Vogel und zieht, flach ihnen fliegend durchs
                    Aufschaun,
weithin das schriftliche Bild seines vereinsamten Schreis. –
Abends führt sie ihn hin zu den Gräbern der Alten
aus dem Klage-Geschlecht, den Sibyllen und Warn-Herrn.   70
Naht aber Nacht, so wandeln sie leiser, und bald
mondets empor, das über Alles
wachende Grab-Mal. Brüderlich jenem am Nil,
der erhabene Sphinx –: der verschwiegenen Kammer
Antlitz.
Und sie staunen dem krönlichen Haupt, das für immer,
schweigend, der Menschen Gesicht
auf die Wage der Sterne gelegt.

Nicht erfaßt es sein Blick, im Frühtod   ╱
schwindelnd. Aber ihr Schaun,   80
hinter dem Pschent-Rand hervor, scheucht es die Eule. Und sie,
streifend im langsamen Abstrich die Wange entlang,
jene der reifesten Rundung,
zeichnet weich in das neue
Totengehör, über ein doppelt
aufgeschlagenes Blatt, den unbeschreiblichen Umriß.

Und höher, die Sterne. Neue. Die Sterne des Leidlands.
Langsam nennt sie die Klage: – Hier,

When at last they arrive in the valley,
an old woman Grief answers a questioning youngster:
Long ago, she tells him, we were a powerful race.
Our ancestors mined the Great Mountains. Among Men you can
            still find
fragments of Griefstone, original pieces our fathers once polished;
...sometimes black anger, petrified slag from the ancient volcano.
Those things were ours. We were prosperous people.

Quietly guiding, she leads the boy
through the wide lands of the Griefs; shows him columns of
            temples,
shows him the ruins of castles, where, long ago,
Grief's lords governed wisely. Shows him the tall tree-of-tears,
fields full of blossoming sadness (we know it only
in earliest leaf...). Shows him Sorrow's beasts grazing.
Sometimes a bird, startled, flashes flat across vision,
scribbles its cry on the distance. At evening she leads him
where sibyls and seers lie buried; shows him the tombs
of the ancients; of the people of Grief.
Night is upon them; ever more softly they move.
Suddenly present, the Sphinx, brother to that by the Nile,
looms like a moon, set to watch over all things –
mute, magisterial, lofty.
They stand in wonder before
the regal head which silently posits, forever,
the face of Mankind in the scales of the stars.

Dazed, still, by dying, his eyes cannot grasp it,
but as she looks, her gaze scares an owl
out from its perch in the sheltering crown.
Gently, its wing, grazing the stone,
feathers the length of the fuller cheek
and for Death's new-sharpened hearing
sketches – as on a page doubly unfolded –
the unrepresentable profile.

And higher yet shine stars of a new kind: the stars
of the Land of the Griefs. One at a time she names them.

siehe: den *Reiter*, den *Stab*, und das vollere Sternbild
nennen sie: *Fruchtkranz*. Dann, weiter, dem Pol zu: 90
Wiege; *Weg*; *Das Brennende Buch*; *Puppe*; *Fenster*.
Aber im südlichen Himmel, rein wie im Innern
einer gesegneten Hand, das klar erglänzende 'M',
das die Mütter bedeutet...–

Doch der Tote muß fort, und schweigend bringt ihn die ältere
Klage bis an die Talschlucht,
wo es schimmert im Mondschein:
die Quelle der Freude. In Ehrfurcht
nennt sie sie, sagt: – Bei den Menschen
ist sie ein tragender Strom. –   100

Stehn am Fuß des Gebirgs.
Und da umarmt sie ihn, weinend.
Einsam steigt er dahin, in die Berge des Urleids.
Und nicht einmal sein Schritt klingt aus dem tonlosen Los.

★

Aber erweckten sie uns, die unendlich Toten, ein Gleichnis,
siehe, sie zeigten vielleicht auf die Kätzchen der leeren
Hasel, die hängenden, oder
meinten den Regen, der fällt auf dunkles Erdreich im Frühjahr. –

Und wir, die an *steigendes* Glück
denken, empfänden die Rührung,   110
die uns beinah bestürzt,
wenn ein Glückliches *fällt*.

See, here is the *Rider*, that one is the *Staff*.
That whole constellation, we call it *Fruit Wreath*.
And then, further over, there by the Pole, those are
Cradle, the *Path*, *Burning Book*, *Puppet* and *Casement*.
But there, in the southern sky, as pure as if drawn
in the palm of a hand that is blessed,
that bright, shining M...
it stands for *The Mothers*.

Time, now, for the dead youth's departure.
In silence the old woman guides him
right to the cleft of the valley –
where the Wellspring of Joy
shines by the light of the moon.
She names it and reverently says:
In the Land of Men this stream
becomes a great river.

At the foot of the mountains they halt.
She embraces him, weeping.
Lonely, his figure ascends and is lost in
the Mountains of Earliest Grief.
No sound of his going comes back from that silence.

★

But those eternally dead might, in ourselves,
awaken some question: perhaps they would point us
to notice the catkins that hang from the leaf-fallen hazel...
refer us to raindrops that fall in the Spring
on dark earth...

And we, unaccustomed to thinking of Fortune except in its rising,
might feel almost perplexed by what moves us
when a happy thing *falls*.

Notes on the Translation

Die erste Elegie

Where the text of the poems is cited in English in the Notes, a literal prose translation is given.

lines

1-10   *Wer, wenn ich schriee, hörte mich denn aus der Engel / Ordnungen?*
The *Elegies* begin with a great cry in the wilderness, and each Elegy will, in its own manner, refer back to this cry.

11   *die findigen Tiere*: English permits an adjective to be made of 'searching' but not of 'finding'.

13-17,   Rilke's partial answers to the great portmanteau questions con-
26-30   cerning human purpose and destiny sometimes come very close to those of Marcel Proust, who was his contemporary. Both men died in their fifty-first year. (Rilke 1875-1926; Proust 1871-1922. See also the note to 11. 49ff of the Seventh Elegy.)

43-45   Gaspara Stampa, a sixteenth-century Italian noblewoman, so transcended the tragic failure of a love affair that her despair was changed to exaltation.
Rilke's enthusiasm for parting, loss, death and bereavement is critical to his particular existentialist credo.

64-65   An inscription in this church, probably the one remembered by Rilke, can be translated as follows:
While I had life I lived for others.
Now after death I have not disappeared
But coldly live in marble for myself.
I once was Willem Hermanus.
Flanders mourns me
Adria sighs for me
And poverty calls me.
Died the 16th October
1593.

66-68   'What they want of me? I am quietly to remove that impression of injustice, which sometimes impedes their pure movement a little.' The young dead have laid on Rilke himself the obliga-tion of preaching that their fate, their early death, is not unjust, is not outrageous.

83-95   The First Elegy ends with the Linos legend: a young god dies and his mourning discovers music. The Elegy has returned once more to the theme of 'value in loss'. But perhaps it also points forward ('can we exist without them?') to some of the matter of the Eighth, Ninth and Tenth Elegies: to the nature of tradition, to the relatedness of past, present, future.

Die zweite Elegie

In the First Elegy, terror of the Angel causes the poet to choke back his cry for help. Here, in the Second, need overcomes dread and the Angels are invoked in spite of his fear and in spite of their dangerousness.

1-6   In the Apocrypha, Tobias sets out on his journey to Rages accompanied by his dog and by the guide, Azarias; who is really the angel Raphael in disguise.

9-17   *Wer seid ihr? . . . in das eigene Antlitz.* One can sense real fear in the question – Who *are* you? Next comes a chain of wonderfully high-flown parentheses which apparently answer the question, describing the Angels themselves. Nevertheless, alone (without Mankind's presence?) these sublime creatures are no more than reflectors of themselves.

27ff   *Aufschaun* can bear the same meaning as *Aufpassen*: it can mean 'to pay attention', 'to be watchful'. In living, in caring, in feeling, we live and care and feel ourselves out of life altogether. As we burn . . . so do we burn out. *Denn Bleiben ist nirgends.* To *be* is to change and, gradually, inexorably, to depart from life.

42-43   *Und alles ist einig, uns zu verschweigen, halb als*
Schande vielleicht und halb als unsägliche Hoffnung.
To the universe, Mankind represents the highest aspirations, and yet also the deepest embarrassment and shame.

57-58   *. . . weil die Stelle nicht schwindet die ihr, Zärtliche/zudeckt . . .*
'. . . because the place does not disappear which you, tender ones, cover. . .' Everything fades. Nothing is permanent. Nothing stays still. 'We know flowering and withering at one and the same time.' (l.16, Fourth Elegy.) Yet, amazingly, Rilke now takes sexual love, takes lovemaking itself, as his theme and begins to preach its permanence, its lastingness, its connections with notions of 'Forever'.

Here, and again at the beginning of the Third Elegy, Rilke succeeds in offering, at one and the same time, chaste metaphor and explicit sexual imagery; and in allowing readers their own choice of interpretation.

Die dritte Elegie

5   *...ehe das Mädchen noch linderte...*: I believe that Rilke here chose to use the verb *lindern* ('to soften') reflexively; which would give a reading: 'even before the maiden softened'. But the line is usually taken to mean: 'even before she has gentled him'.

All action and drive are given to the Lord of Desire himself: the role of the young woman is entirely subordinate.

8   *O des Blutes Neptun*: Britannia herself, Drake, Nelson and others have appropriated 'Neptune' so thoroughly in English folklore that I have thought it best to leave the god anonymous, here. Furthermore, Rilke's 'river-god of the blood' of line 2 has become the 'Neptune of the blood' of line 8, and to render him a 'water-god' in each case would be to interfere even more than I have done.

20   *...doch ältere Schrecken...*: the 'mixed exaltation and terror' of Graves's White Goddess; of sexual love and of Muse-poetry?

26   *Mutter, du machtest ihn klein...*: probably the intended meaning, the heavier meaning, is 'Mother, you made him when he was little'. But *klein machen* may be used idiomatically as meaning 'to belittle', and there is a Rilke poem full of mother-hatred written in 1915 (*Ach wehe, meine Mutter reisst mich ein*) which suggests that the double meaning is not accidental.

49-63   At the beginning of the Third Elegy there is *die Geliebte*, the beloved maiden. In the next section, the female presence changes to that of the young mother: the slender, graceful and all-capable protectress. Next, at line 58, the boy has to descend into the ravine where various horrors await him (*das Furchtbare, jedes Schreckliche, das Entsetzliche*). According to Graves, Maiden, Mother and Night Mare are all manifestations of the Triple Goddess: the source of all Muse-poetry.

81ff   Translated literally it would have to be: 'O quietly, quietly, do something loving before him, a reliable daily task...'

The 'garden' probably stands for 'Nature controlled and made human' – against the jungles, the teeming sexual wilderness of the earlier scenes.

Die vierte Elegie

The Fourth, the bitterest and least reconciled of the Elegies, was written in Munich during 1915. Like the Eighth Elegy to which it stands closely related, the Fourth is written in blank verse. In both these Elegies, the rational and self-conscious vacillations of Mankind are contrasted with the bone-marrow sureness of the natural world.

In the end, Rilke's *Elegies* are – perhaps only by a hairsbreadth – poems of affirmation. A bitterly hardwon affirmation, given extra force by its passage through deserts of despair. This Elegy addresses itself primarily to those deserts.

1-18   Fish in the unruffled lakes
Their swarming colours wear,
Swans in the winter air
A white perfection have,
And the great lion walks
Through his innocent grove;
Lion, fish and swan
Act and are gone
Upon Time's toppling wave.

We, till shadowed days are done,
We must weep and sing
Duty's conscious wrong,
The Devil in the clock,
The goodness carefully worn
For atonement or good luck;
We must lose our loves,
On each beast and bird that moves
Turn an envious look.

(From 'Song of the Beggars', V, 1936, W.H. Auden, *Collected Poems*, 1976.) Auden's lines provide echo and a lovely exegesis for Rilke's opening of this Elegy.

It is worth comparing the *Feindschaft ist uns das Nächste* of lines 10 and 11 of the Fourth Elegy with the *gegenüber sein und nichts als das und immer gegenüber* of the Eighth Elegy. But there is an even stronger echo in *Gegenstrophen*, the so-called *Frauen-elegie* which originally stood in the place of the present Fifth Elegy:

> *Wir, von uns selber gekränkt,*
> *Kränkende gern, und gern*
> *Wiedergekränkte aus Not.*
> *Wir, wie Waffen, dem Zorn*
> *neben dem Schlaf gelegt.*

> We – by our own selves injured,
> ready to injure; ready and needing
> in turn to be injured.

> We – who are weapons as ready
> to anger as sleep.

27ff   *Puppe* can mean 'doll' or 'puppet' (as well as the 'pupa' of an insect.) Rilke is here concerned with the stage and with performance, so that 'puppet' would seem the better choice. 'Puppet' more or less contains 'doll'; whereas 'doll' has no room for the other word's vocation as actor.

      'Grace appears most purely in that human form in which consciousness is either non-existent or infinite.' (Heinrich von Kleist, *Essay on the Marionette Theatre*, 1810). Here as elsewhere, Rilke questions the relations between men and Angels, children and adults, between animals and mankind, objects and living creatures, the living and the dead. The questions tend to ask: What of this is real? What stays less than real? What might progress *beyond* the real; transcend it?

35   'that boy with the squinting brown eye' is Egon von Rilke, Rilke's beloved cousin who died in childhood and to whom the Eighth Sonnet in Part Two of the *Sonnets to Orpheus* is dedicated. He appears also in Rilke's autobiographical novel, *Malte Laurids Brigge*.

85   *unbeschreiblich* means 'indescribable'. But the word is perhaps most often used in the sense of 'indescribably awful'; 'appalling'; 'terrible'.

Die fünfte Elegie

Of all the *Elegies*, the Fifth is the one whose content is most arguably about 'art' as much as about 'life'.

Gegenstrophen, the original Fifth Elegy, was ultimately withdrawn from the Duino cycle and survives as a poem on its own. The present Fifth Elegy, Elegie des Saltimbanques as Rilke sometimes called it, was completed on 14 February 1922 – some days after the letters in which he excitedly announced that he had 'completed' the *Elegies*.

The Fifth is outstandingly the most modern of the *Elegies*, the most arbitrary and the freest in its form. Nevertheless, many lines are trochaic or dactylic pentameters or hexameters, and such lines come and go throughout the Elegy:

niémáls zŭ/fríedĕnĕr/Wíllĕ?// Sońdĕrn ĕr/wríngt sǐe . . .

In 1915 Rilke lived for several months in the Munich house of Frau Hertha Koenig, to whom this Elegy is dedicated: the great Picasso painting of 1905, *Les Saltimbanques*, was his companion during this time. But another source for Rilke was a group of street entertainers, once led by Père Rollin the weightlifter, demoted in his old age to drummer. The group, which performed in the Luxembourg Gardens during the years in which Rilke was in Paris, may well have provided Picasso with his subject.

Of the six figures of *Les Saltimbanques*, only the older boy, the youth, is not addressed or discussed as an individual in Rilke's poem. The others appear as follows:

The old man, the weightlifter, in lines 26-32
The young man, in lines 33-35
The boy, in lines 40-57
The young woman, the mother, briefly in lines 47-48
The little girl, in lines 62-72

12-14   *des Dastehns/grosser Anfangsbuchstab . . .*: 'the great initial letter of Existence . . .' The figures in the Picasso painting are so placed that they loosely describe the letter D. 'Existence' would lose the reference to the painting's format (probably there by intention). 'Durance' would be an awful equivalent, a non-equivalent, for *Dastehn*. But 'Destiny' gives a close match in sound, bears the essential D and is a first cousin in sense to *Dastehn*: whatever 'exists' may do so because 'Destiny' intends or permits it.

18-25   The 'focus' or 'centre' is the group of performers; a 'rose' which has the onlookers, the spectators gathering and departing, for its 'petals'. In their midst, the acrobat rises and falls like a piston – or stands like the pistil of a flower. But the 'rose' will never come to genuine fruition: its pollen is *Unlust*, its fertility a sham fertility. *Unlust* is difficult to translate satisfactorily: 'listlessness', its closest English equivalent semantically, is far too weak on its own. *Lust* can stand for 'appetite, pleasure, fun, lust, interest, desire, wish' – although not one of these words fits it entirely. *Unlust* stands for a cancelled appetite; a neutrality or an aversion, a negative hunger. 'Satiety'?

33   *. . . der Sohn eines Nackens . . .*: 'neck' is synechdoche. In *Les Saltimbanques*, the robust male figure in the harlequin suit stands with shoulders, head and neck locked rigid, as if made in one piece.

58-61   *Engel! . . . 'Subrisio Saltat.'* Rilke appeals to the Angel to preserve the child-acrobat's professional smile; to put it away in a jar (labelled in Latin like the medicinal jars of old-fashioned pharmicists – Acrobat's Smile). Is this enthusiasm to be taken at face value, or is it irony? We are still in the grip of 'performance'.

73-80,   Between incompetence on the one hand and over-competence,
81-86   sheer slickness, on the other, the difficult may – riskily – be attempted and sometimes achieved. It is here that 'performance' may become 'art' – and 'art' become 'reality'.

94-106   The Angel is finally invoked once more. This time there can be no suspicion of any ironic undertone. Might there be a place or a time in which human love and human virtuosity would find themselves completed and fulfilled; transcending life, time and death?

Die sechste Elegie

1-4 'The Fig is somewhat distinct in its fructification. It has no visible flowers, and many persons have consequently imagined that none was borne by the Fig. As a matter of fact it does bear flowers, but they are not externally visible on the branches. They are really concealed within the fleshy bodies which we call the fruit.' (T.W. Sanders, *Fruit and its Cultivation*, London, n.d.)

By the autumn, the fruitlets which may ripen into the figs themselves are already minutely present – 'determined' – but they will not normally ripen until the late summer of the following year.

16 *denen der gärtnernde Tod anders die Adern verbiegt.*
'Whose veins gardening Death twists differently.'
I have interfered a little with Rilke's metaphors here, in attempting to make his image and its expression credible in English.

17, *Lächeln*: 'Smiles, smiling' are laden with meaning for Rilke in
44 this Elegy as also in the Second, Third and Fifth Elegies. 'Smile' is to Rilke rather as 'honey' is to Shakespeare: a sweetness not always to be trusted. Here, in line 17, the Hero overtakes smiling, leaves it behind him. At the end of the Elegy he stands at the end of the smiles: has survived them.

Die siebente Elegie

The Fourth Elegy is bitter and regretful almost without relief. This, the Seventh, is not without its bitterness, ironies and reservations, but it is all the same a poem of celebration and of affirmation. It is *bejahend*: it is yea-saying!

'Life is nothing...' preaches the Sixth Elegy; 'exemplary is the Hero, who holds it cheap.'

'Living is marvellous!' sings the Seventh, and proceeds to exalt the senses, the world itself, life, nature, art, architecture and tradition.

1ff *Werbung nicht mehr...* 'No more wooing...' sternly orders the poet; who then woos for fifty brilliant lines, describing what he proscribes.

36 *das Dichte der Kindheit*: *Dichte* may mean 'density' as a physicist uses the word, but here it seems to stand for the pressing reality

of the senses in childhood. For the sheer *taste* of everything, while we are still young.

It is just possible that *das Dichte der Kindheit* is to be set against the later *das Offene der Kreatur*, in the Eighth Elegy. If so, the bomb has a very long fuse.

49ff In Rilke's credo, tradition has a mystical dimension: it is necessary (it is, indeed, our *Auftrag*, our mission in life) to transform the visible into the invisible, artefacts into a culture, happenings into experience, into a tradition... so that all these shall finally come together into a universe of the spirit (including paradoxically, the spirits of objects; the animism of *things*). This piety of Rilke's has all the significance of Proust's recollection – across a lifetime – of the flavour of the madeleine, of the touch of a linen napkin, the uneven cobblestones of the Guermantes courtyard. ('This explained why it was that my anxiety on the subject of my death had ceased at the moment when I had unconsciously recognised the taste of the little madeleine, since the being which at that moment I had been was an extra-temporal being...' '...had made it possible for my being to secure... what normally it never apprehends: a fragment of time in the pure state.' (Marcel Proust, *Time Regained*, London 1970. *Le Temps Retrouvé*, Paris 1927.)

52-62 *Wo einmal ein dauerndes Haus war*... It is worth contrasting the tone of voice of lines 1-29 of this Elegy, which take naturism as their subject, with that of these lines which turn towards functionalism, rationalism, modernism, and (surely!) are preaching with restrained fury against them.

Rilke is here almost certainly making bitter war on The Modern. It is believed that he hated and feared all those drawing-board-setsquare-ferroconcrete-powerhouse ideals which he thought of as 'American', and that his prejudice included England which had, after all, been Castle Dracula to the monster of the Industrial Revolution – and would later nurture the utopian horrors of 'Metroland'. *Zeitgeist* (the spirit or genius which marks the thought or feeling of a period or age, OED) has passed into the English language. *Kraft* and *spannender Drang* seem to be sketching 'electricity'... the wind in 'American' sails. (See Eudo C. Mason, *Rilke, Europe and the English Speaking World*, Cambridge 1961, p.155 and pp.179-86.)

63ff Rilke returns yet again to the theme of 'tradition': of our duty to serve as its builders and custodians. Human function and purpose (*Auftrag*!) is to experience, to preserve (through witnessing? by saying?) and thus to immortalise and to transcend. Human propriety depends on the preservation of a living continuity, a tradition.

Metre, diction and content are rapidly becoming harsher, less regular, more hermetic. The Elegy's coda is, I believe intentionally, elusive; difficult and demanding in interpretation: *Unfasslich*.

Die achte Elegie

Unlike the others in the cycle, Elegies Four and Eight are written in iambic pentameters. They are related in content as well as in form, although there are differences in mood between them. The Fourth Elegy remains bitter throughout in its feeling of isolation and in its echoing sense of loss. But in the Eighth there is perhaps (for poet and reader, both?) a sombre happiness in the poetic expression of sadness, of regret, of difficulty.

The Elegy is dedicated to Rudolf Kassner, a friend and contemporary and the mystagogue by whom Rilke was profoundly influenced; although probably without becoming fully converted to Kassner's beliefs. Its theme is in part an Old Testament theme: that of the Fruit of the Tree of Knowledge and of the expulsion of mankind from Eden. Rilke believes that we are disinherited, partly by our self-awareness and by the contentious nature of the human will, from the place in the universe which the simpler creatures enjoy unquestioningly. And it is the knowledge of our own mortality and the importance we ascribe to it that makes us, finally, the outcasts that we are: *Wir sind nicht einig*. The second line of the Fourth Elegy has become the Argument of the Eighth.

1ff   *Die Kreatur* is not easy to translate: Rilke's 'Creation' has no Creator. (D.H. Lawrence's book, *Birds, Beasts and Flowers*, a title which might pass into German as *Die Kreatur*, was published in the same year as the Rilke *Elegies*.)

      das Offene: Here, the first meaning is perhaps 'open space' – but it may just as well mean: 'open chance, open option, choice, the unforeseen, the unforeclosed'. As so often, Rilke seems at pains to allow a word or a phrase to drift from one meaning to another or to point to several meanings at once.

      Tier: 'Animal' is the obvious equivalent, yet the word has two extra syllables and it makes a very different kind of sound. 'Brute' seems too archaic as well as too brutal; 'beast' is too close to 'beastly' and to 'bestial'. Yet, English does not offer 'creatures' as a clear antonym to 'mankind'.

17-19   *und niemals Nirgends ohne Nicht*: 'and never (that) nowhere without "not"...' The 'nowhere' can be unpacked as meaning, at the same time, 'everywhere': never-never land as 'ever-ever land' – a nirvana of place (and time), free from prohibitions, free from supervision, free from limitation, from negatives.

19-21   *Als Kind...gerüttelt*: 'As a child one loses oneself in this, in silence, and one is shaken'.

The word *gerüttelt* may here mean 'rocked' or 'jogged' as a baby is rocked, to soothe it. But it may just as well mean the opposite. Dandled? Or rattled? Given the mood of the Eighth Elegy, the poor child has most likely been shaken *from* its bliss.

32-42   Rilke returns, here, to some of the matter of the Fourth Elegy.

52-55   *O Seligkeit der* kleinen *Kreatur,*
die immer bleibt im Schoosse, der sie austrug;
o Glück der Mücke, die noch innen hüpft,
selbst wenn sie Hochzeit hat: denn Schooss ist alles.
The assonances of line 54 (*Glück/Mücke/hüpft*) make for a kind of gnat-sound; the line dances up and down like the insects themselves.
Hochzeit: marriage, wedding day, nuptial. Dismantled it becomes 'high-time'; as one says 'heyday', 'high days and holidays'. Rilke's picture of 'the little creature . . . in its heyday . . . leaping in the womb', is unexpected and disarming in the midst of the dark tones of this Elegy.
denn Schooss ist Alles: a typically Rilkean construction which might offer either or both of two readings:
i) . . . for womb is all things
ii) . . . for all things are womb (for it)

55-60   Rilke's text is firmly constructed and his images will often bear very literal examination. Mammals, the 'warm animals', can never wholly overcome their sadness, their nostalgia for their first home: the womb, the primal Eden. The 'little creatures', the insects, emerge from the egg directly into the elements: the world is their womb. The birds share some of this womb-is-all-things inheritance with the insects (they *almost* know it; as they almost know the open and the closed, the earth and the sky, life and death). But they are also given the nest-womb, presided over by the presence, in the fledgling's own image, of the parent bird. (The free Etruscan soul; the stone sarcophagus; the figure above it which both presides and imprisons.)

70-75   'Then, who has turned us around so that, whatever we do, we bear the attitude of one who is departing? As he, upon the final hill which one more time lets him see all his valley, turns, pauses, lingers – so do we live, and ever take our leave.'
Blühn und verdorrn ist uns zugleich bewusst: Line 6, the Fourth Elegy. 'We're at the same time conscious of blossoming and withering.' Man, says Rilke in the Fourth and Eighth Elegies, never lays aside his knowledge that his own life is finite. 'We never have, not for a single day, pure space before us in which the flowers endlessly open. Always it is World . . .'

Die neunte Elegie

Rilke returns to the themes of the previous Elegy. We might choose to live as acceptingly, as decently, in experience as does *die Kreatur*. Instead, we perversely choose to involve ourselves with notions of fate – to meddle in our destinies and with Destiny itself. Why? These are among Rilke's most lasting preoccupations. Thesis: 'All experience is yours; submit; accept; transcend.' Antithesis: 'Make your own destiny; accept nothing; never rest; life itself is restless movement.' And the synthesis? It is perhaps stated more clearly in the Ninth than anywhere else in the *Elegies*.

10-16   *Aber dieses... scheint nicht widerrufbar*: Here again is the affirmation, *Hiersein ist herrlich*, of the Seventh Elegy. The experience of a mortal life is indestructible, eternal, *im*mortal. Our own experience is far less frail, less fleeting than we believe it. We ourselves, ephemeral though we may be, are unique, heraldic, and also necessary to the whole.

45ff   *Tun ohne Bild...*: there may be at least three different levels of meaning in this passage.

      i) 'Action without picture' might stand for functionalism, indifferent to image. Near at hand lie 'mass-production'; 'electricity'.

      ii) Or the phrase might signify 'forms without precedent' – that is, outside any established tradition.

      iii) Rilke is, however, a poet: his 'action' is through words. In this context, *ohne Bild* might mean 'words with not enough behind them', 'words that are no more than wordy'; might mean 'cliché'. And this meaning would refer us back to the previous section, the one concerned with 'saying'.

52-56   The lines reaffirm the magic and the relevance of *World*, of our own world at its simplest and Earthliest, undecorated by any ineffable pretensions. We are also reminded to listen for the heartbeat of *things*... eloquent, made in our own image, a part of our experience, just as we are part of theirs.

67-69   *Preise dem Engel die Welt, nicht die unsägliche...*   (Ninth Elegy)
         Nirgends, Geliebte, wird Welt sein als innen.   (Seventh Elegy)
         Hiersein ist herrlich.   (Seventh Elegy)
    It is as if these three distinct statements of affirmation had been plaited together to bring the Ninth Elegy to triumphant conclusion.

Die zehnte Elegie

There is a strong connection between the first and the last Elegies of the Duino cycle. *Wer, wenn ich schriee...* and *Das ich dereinst...* introduce their respective Elegies in similar tones of invocation, and the death of Linos at the end of the First Elegy is recalled as the footsteps of the dead youth go forever into the Mountains of Primal Grief, in the Tenth.

1-2   Perhaps surprisingly, the opening of the Tenth Elegy contains some complicated word-play:
          Ausgang/Ein*sicht*: out/in
          auf*singe*/zu*stimmend* contains:
      i) *auf*/*zu*, open/closed
      ii) *singend*/*stimmend*, singing/sounding,
which resemble one another in sound as in sense. In other words they assent to, are in assonance with one another; which is what *zustimmend* means.

13   *unser winterwähriges Laub, unser dunkeles Sinngrün,*
'Green' tends to bear a more positive symbolism in German than in English. Often it stands for 'freshness', 'life', 'hope', although it can, as in English, also stand for 'unripe', 'unready'. The Ninth Elegy began with the green of the laurel among other kinds of green, and in the Third Elegy there was the *lichtgrün* of the boy's not-so-innocent heart.

14-15   *nicht zur Zeit, – sind Stelle*: It is worth noting the manner in which Rilke converts 'time' into 'place' here. In the next section (*den Trostmarkt den die Kirche begrenzt*) it is a state of belief which has become 'place'.

16ff   *leiden* together with *trösten, klagen, hiersein, dasein, einsehen, kümmern*: words like these weighty, abstract German verbs and their associated nouns seem to defy transposition into an appropriate English. For *die Gassen der Leidstadt*, neither 'City of Pain' nor 'City of Sorrow' will quite do, for although they are mechanically correct they do not express what Rilke seems to have intended. *Die Leidstadt* is found to be full of memorials and statuary, gilded bombast, and stocked with ready-made consolations and palliatives. Rilke's text here seems to be concerned not with death itself, but with the rituals with which our early century responded to that event. Tall hats, crêpe bands, black veils, elm boards and brass handles: the whole institution and apparatus of Mourning.

23ff   A shift in mood accompanies the appearance of the fairground on the outskirts of the *Leidstadt*. Now, after the high diction of the Elegy's opening, Rilke places us firmly in the first quarter of the twentieth century; among hoardings and fun-fairs, branded goods and beer and skittles. If we sniff, we can smell the low-octane petrol; if we listen, hear motor-horns; perhaps a biplane droning overhead.

wo és/záppelt/vŏn Zíel/únd sích/bléchĕrn/bĕnímmt,
The stresses tapdance like the mannikins they describe. *Blechern*
is 'tinny' – but the impression given by these lines is brassy;
cheapjack but also frightening. Macheath may be somewhere
nearby.

33-37   A long parenthesis interrupts the voice which has begun to tell
us 'where it is . . . really'. We are shown hoardings advertising
extremely nasty beer, with *Zerstreuungen* (crisps of a sort,
perhaps?) to match. *Todlos*, the brand name of the beer, may
signify either 'deathless' or, alternatively (or at one and the
same time) 'death-fated'.

38ff   . . . *ists wirklich*: here, 'where it's *real*', the tone changes again,
switching from the voice of the huckster to that of the story-
teller – to the voice of legend. *Hĭntĕr/íhr hér/kómmt ĕr ĭn/Wíĕsĕn./*
Sĭe săgt . . . It is as if, within the space of forty lines of verse, Rilke
had thrown his voice from the intonations of the *Book of Common
Prayer* to those of *The Waste Land* – and then back again into the
language of legend and of parable (Bunyan, perhaps).

There is something of Seurat's *La Grande Jatte* in the picture
of children, lovers, dogs playing on the seedy urban turf. But
Rilke's painting is less classical and measured, more German
Expressionist.

40-52   *eine junge Klage*: *Klage* is perhaps the most difficult of the 'per-
sonifications' of the *Duino Elegies*. Langenscheidt gives – com-
plaint; grievance; lamentation. But a direct translation seems
to give shamblingly inadequate solutions. 'Lament' (the usual
translation of *Klage* in English versions of the Elegies) somehow
does not have the right sound or size, and the personification
sits uncomfortably upon it. Something seems to suggest that a
short and rather harsh-sounding word is necessary ('tern'
makes the right kind of sound; 'cormorant' doesn't). A word is
needed which can carry the weight and dignity of sorrow, yet
without sounding maudlin or Pre-Raphaelitish. 'Grief' seems
to me to carry the right tone, both as sound and as sense (although
it has the sense of *Klage* only at one remove, only by means of
a backwards jump from the concept of 'grievance'). Whatever
the word, it has to be a name as well: the clan-name of the young
woman, the name of her country as well as that of her 'noble
ancestry'.

48-54   The Grief maiden is now dropped from the narrative and her
place taken by a youth, by a particular young man; *not* the young
man from the fairground who first followed the maiden, but
one of the 'young dead'. He appears, without introduction,
as 'the youth' in line 54, and is immediately taken up and

101

befriended by a female Elder of the tribe of the Griefs. This relationship, between green young man and grey wise-woman, continues virtually until the end of this, the final Elegy.

55-59   'We – spendthrifts of Sorrow' was a theme at the beginning of the Tenth, and here Rilke briefly takes it up again. The fragments of those under-prized sorrows are valued now: they have become 'antiques'.

60-78   The *Landschaft der Klagen* seemed likely to be related to Egypt (more than any other the 'Land of the Dead'). Here, now, is the statement of its kinship with the land of the Nile and with its Sphinx.

There is a line break between the words, but *Kammer Antlitz* is normally used to mean 'chamber-face' in the sense of 'privy-councillor's face', 'politician's face'. If the Gods played poker, is this how they might look?

82-86   In line 68, Rilke converted (synaesthetically: sound into graphic gesture into sight) a bird's cry into calligraphy. In *these* lines, the pinions of the owl scan the contour of part of the great sculpture and, as if by radar or sonar, its shape can be 'heard' by the dead youth.

doppelt aufgeschlagenes Blatt: a neat and literal description of doubled-over facing pages in a book; when opened out they make a four-page spread.

109ff   *Glück*: the German word is neither quite 'fortune', nor is it as random (and light-weight?) as mere 'luck'. 'Felicity' is nearer, or would be if it were not too latinate and much too old-fashioned; whereas 'happiness' is probably too bland and certainly too long. The German word is a kind of amalgam of 'luck', 'joy', 'happiness' and 'fortune'.

Duineser Elegien